Academic Freedom in American Higher Education:
Rights, Responsibilities, and Limitations

by Robert K. Poch

ASHE-ERIC Higher Education Report No. 4, 1993

Prepared by

Clearinghouse on Higher Education
The George Washington University

In cooperation with

Association for the Study
of Higher Education

Published by

School of Education and Human Development
The George Washington University

Jonathan D. Fife, Series Editor

Cite as
Poch, Robert K. 1993. *Academic Freedom in American Higher Education: Rights, Responsibilities, and Limitations.* ASHE-ERIC Higher Education Report No. 4. Washington, D.C.: The George Washington University, School of Education and Human Development.

Library of Congress Catalog Card Number 93-61674
ISSN 0884-0040
ISBN 1-878380-25-9

Managing Editor: Bryan Hollister
Manuscript Editor: Alexandra Rockey
Cover design by Michael David Brown, Rockville, Maryland

The ERIC Clearinghouse on Higher Education invites individuals to submit proposals for writing monographs for the *ASHE-ERIC Higher Education Report* series. Proposals must include:
1. A detailed manuscript proposal of not more than five pages.
2. A chapter-by-chapter outline.
3. A 75-word summary to be used by several review committees for the initial screening and rating of each proposal.
4. A vita and a writing sample.

ERIC **Clearinghouse on Higher Education**
School of Education and Human Development
The George Washington University
One Dupont Circle, Suite 630
Washington, DC 20036-1183

This publication was prepared partially with funding from the Office of Educational Research and Improvement, U.S. Department of Education, under contract no. ED RI-88-062014. The opinions expressed in this report do not necessarily reflect the positions or policies of OERI or the Department.

EXECUTIVE SUMMARY

Academic freedom provides the foundation for faculty scholarship and teaching. The ability to exchange ideas and concepts freely in the classroom, to explore and disseminate new knowledge and to speak professionally and as a private citizen are essential elements for the intellectual vitality of a college or university. It is important, therefore, that faculty members and higher education administrators understand the meaning, content, legal parameters, and contemporary issues that pertain to and affect academic freedom in American higher education.

This report synthesizes academic freedom literature and applicable case law to provide a succinct look at the current issues and contexts surrounding academic freedom. In doing so, the following major questions are posed and addressed.

What Are Popular Notions of Academic Freedom?
Conceptions of academic freedom existed in America from the first establishment of American colleges in the 17th century. However, it was not until the American Association of University Professors (AAUP) and the Association of American Colleges (AAC) developed jointly the 1940 Statement of Academic Freedom and Tenure that a popular notion of academic freedom existed in the United States. The 1940 Statement specified those elements which together comprised academic freedom for college and university faculty—namely, the freedom to teach, research, and publish, and to speak extramurally.

The large number of professional organizations and societies which later endorsed the 1940 Statement elevated it to a position of prominence in the academic community. By virtue of the volume of endorsements and the statement's subsequent recognition by the courts as being the standard professional definition of academic freedom, the 1940 Statement achieved status as the popular notion of academic freedom in America.

Is Academic Freedom a Legal Right?
While numerous parallels exist between the freedoms specified in the 1940 Statement and the First and 14th amendments of the Constitution, the U.S. Supreme Court has never granted academic freedom full constitutional status. As citizens, public college and university faculty members enjoy the same rights and privileges as other citizens, and their institutions are obli-

gated to respect those rights. However, faculty members are obligated by professional standards to conduct themselves in ways that reflect respect for students, administrators, and other members of their academic communities. While faculty members can exercise the same constitutional freedoms as other citizens, they are responsible also for the maintenance of the professional standards and expectations of their disciplines and institutions.

Do Faculty at Private Institutions Have the Same Rights as Faculty at Public Institutions?

While faculty members at public colleges and universities enjoy constitutional protection, faculty at private institutions must rely mainly upon contractual safeguards which may or may not include equivalent protections. The content of faculty contracts in private colleges and universities forms, in short, the limitations and freedoms available for intellectual inquiry. It is important, therefore, that faculty contracts in independent institutions address the four primary components of the AAUP 1940 Statement on Academic Freedom.

What Current Issues Affect Academic Freedom?

As described in this report, current issues that significantly affect academic freedom include artistic expression, political correctness, limitations initiated by church-related colleges and universities, and subpoenaed research information. While the AAUP provides some policy guidance on current challenging academic freedom issues, it does not provide specific policy guidance on political correctness, as the organization does not perceive it to be a threat to faculty academic freedom.

In the absence of an organizationally endorsed policy statement, it is important for the institutions themselves to consider carefully the potential effect of the issue and, where appropriate, to develop an internal policy statement in the interest of preserving academic freedom. Moreover, the AAUP's 1970 interpretive comment on church-related colleges implies that the AAUP knows definitively if church-related colleges and universities need a departure from academic freedom as defined by the association; the comment does not reflect consideration of the possibility that different constructions of "truth" and "ways of knowing" exist in academe.

A review of the literature contained in this report suggests that:

- Faculty should be involved actively in the development of institutional policies on issues that affect academic freedom.
- Colleges and universities should develop clear artistic and educational guidelines regarding the selection of artistic works that are displayed on campus. Artistic expression that conveys political or social thought is given a higher level of constitutional protection than "art for art's sake." Institutions can designate an alternate site for the display of sexually explicit, but not obscene, material.
- In addressing "political correctness," college and university faculty manuals and student publications should state that diversity of opinion, ethnic backgrounds, and individual human experiences are valued elements of academic freedom. Moreover, institutions should state clearly in faculty and student documents that while the freedom to express ideas and beliefs will be respected, conduct and behavior that result in the defacement of property, physical intimidation of others, or the disruption of campus activities will be subject to penalty.

What Conclusions and Implications Can be Derived from Contemporary Academic Freedom Issues and Contexts?

At the core of the academic freedom issues and contexts described in this report is the importance of clear and precise faculty policy statements which address what freedoms are available and what role faculty should play when potentially competing issues arise. Specifically:

- Public and independent colleges and universities should include in faculty handbooks an official policy statement on academic freedom that specifies what freedoms are available to faculty members.
- If an institution endorses the AAUP 1940 Statement of Principles on Academic Freedom and Tenure, the statement should be printed in full in the faculty handbook and referenced in the teaching contract. Moreover, the institution should indicate whether it endorses also the AAUP 1970 Interpretive Comments.
- Any restrictions on academic freedom should be stated clearly and completely in the faculty handbook and ref-

erenced in the teaching contract.

- Church-related colleges and universities should make a special effort to specify for faculty members limitations on academic freedom, including restrictions resulting from doctrinal tenets.

ADVISORY BOARD

Barbara E. Brittingham
The University of Rhode Island

Jay L. Chronister
University of Virginia

Carol Everly Floyd
Board of Regents of the Regency Universities System
State of Illinois

Rodolfo Z. Garcia
Michigan State University

Elizabeth M. Hawthorne
University of Toledo

L. Jackson Newell
University of Utah

Barbara Taylor
Association of Governing Boards of Universities and Colleges

Barbara S. Plakens
Iowa State University

William Rittenberg
Michigan State University

Karen Spear
Fort Lewis College

Kala Stroop
Southeast Missouri State University

John M. Swales
The University of Michigan

Ellen Switkes
University of California–Oakland

James J. Szablewicz
Mapp, Mapp & Klein, Attorneys at Law

Jo Taylor
Wayne State University

William G. Tierney
The Pennsylvania State University

Kathryn Towns
The Pennsylvania State University–Harrisburg

Caroline Turner
University of Minnesota–Twin Cities

Elizabeth A. Williams
University of Massachuetts–Amherst

REVIEW PANEL

Charles Adams
University of Massachusetts-Amherst

Louis Albert
American Association for Higher Education

Richard Alfred
University of Michigan

Philip G. Altbach
State University of New York-Buffalo

Marilyn J. Amey
University of Kansas

Louis C. Attinasi, Jr.
University of Houston

Robert J. Barak
Iowa State Board of Regents

Alan Bayer
Virginia Polytechnic Institute and State University

John P. Bean
Indiana University

Louis W. Bender
Florida State University

John M. Braxton
Vanderbilt University

Peter McE. Buchanan
Council for Advancement and
  Support of Education

John A. Centra
Syracuse University

Arthur W. Chickering
George Mason University

Shirley M. Clark
Oregon State System of Higher Education

Darrel A. Clowes
Virginia Polytechnic Institute and State University

John W. Creswell
University of Nebraska-Lincoln

Deborah DiCroce
Piedmont Virginia Community College

Richard Duran
University of California

Kenneth C. Green
University of Southern California

Edward R. Hines
Illinois State University

Marsha W. Krotseng
West Virginia State College and University Systems

George D. Kuh
Indiana University–Bloomington

Daniel T. Layzell
University of Wisconsin System

Meredith Ludwig
American Association of State Colleges and Universities

Mantha V. Mehallis
Florida Atlantic University

Robert J. Menges
Northwestern University

Toby Milton
Essex Community College

James R. Mingle
State Higher Education Executive Officers

Gary Rhoades
University of Arizona

G. Jeremiah Ryan
Harford Community College

Daryl G. Smith
Claremont Graduate School

William Tierney
The Pennsylvania State University

Susan Twombly
University of Kansas

Harold Wechsler
University of Rochester

Michael J. Worth
The George Washington University

CONTENTS

FOREWORD

In *The Law of Higher Education*, William Kaplin introduces faculty academic freedom:

> *The concept of academic freedom eludes precise definition. It is a concept that draws from both the world of education and the world of law. Courts have increasingly used academic freedom as the catch-all term to describe the legal rights and responsibilities of the teaching profession. This judicial conception of academic freedom is essentially an attempt to reconcile basic constitutional principles with the prevailing views of academic freedom's social and intellectual role in American life* (1985, p. 180).

Thus, the concept of academic freedom has legal implications and represents fundamental beliefs that help to define the role of the faculty. The concept of academic freedom serves higher education well when the understanding of what the concept represents is consistent. However, when conflict clouds this understanding or when the concept starts to represent values that are not legally supportable and may even contradict the mission of the institution, the concept no longer serves its purpose.

The shield of academic freedom often is raised by faculty members when they feel threatened. They use this shield to protect their rights to control the curriculum, the content of a course, and the pursuit of controversial research. Sometimes the threats are real; sometimes the shield is used to protect the faculty from accountability and the realities of fiscal constraints.

Two areas are important to institutions and faculty in making the concept of academic freedom a positive force within an institution's culture. First is understanding the legal realities of academic freedom. Second is understanding what academic freedom means for an individual institution—a meaning that reaches beyond the legal definition. It is this factor that is unique to each institution and creates confusion and distrust.

In this report by Robert K. Poch, associate commissioner at the South Carolina Commission on Higher Education, academic freedom is discussed—first, in general terms from a historical context. Then, specific contemporary issues are examined. The author has identified four areas of concern: issues surrounding artistic expression, political correctness, academic freedom within church-related colleges, and protection of sources of information used for research. These issues will dominate the discussion of academic freedom throughout this decade.

The concept of academic freedom is fundamental not only to the essence of American higher education but to our democratic society as well. As was stated in *Keyishian v. Board of Regents*:

Our nation is deeply committed to safeguarding academic freedom, which is of transcendent value to all of us and not merely to the teachers concerned (Kaplin 1985, p. 182).

It is the responsibility of all involved in the academy to refrain from taking academic freedom for granted and to be aware of situations in which this freedom truly is threatened. Robert Poch's report is one element in a continuous effort to maintain this vigilance.

Jonathan D. Fife
Series Editor, Professor of Higher Education Administration, and Director, ERIC Clearinghouse on Higher Education

ACKNOWLEDGMENTS

This monograph would not have been possible without the love, support, and understanding of my wife Cindy and the two most patient children on the face of the earth, Christy and Erik. All three gave up weekends and evenings and tried hard (sometimes successfully) to keep the house quiet. To them, I give my deepest love and gratitude.

INTRODUCTION

Academic freedom is one of the most valued components of higher education in the United States. Upon it rests the active discourse, critical debate, free exchange of ideas, and communication of values that characterize effective scholarship, teaching, and learning. This report examines the historical emergence, definition, and meaning of academic freedom; its legal parameters in public and independent institutions; and current issues that can, and do, affect academic freedom in higher education institutions throughout the country.

Challenges to academic freedom will not fade away.

While the American Association of University Professors (AAUP) and the Association of American Colleges (AAC) set forth in the 1940 Statement of Principles on Academic Freedom and Tenure the basic components of faculty academic freedom—namely, the freedom to teach, research, publish, and speak extramurally—many challenges to academic freedom arise for which faculty and institutional leaders must be prepared. Preparation involves understanding the meaning and value of academic freedom so that faculty and policy makers may act with conviction when challenges to intellectual liberty materialize. Moreover, institutional leaders must understand the policy implications of academic freedom in order to make informed decisions in the course of daily college and university administration and when serious policy issues arise.

This report focuses on some of the most difficult contemporary academic freedom-related issues confronting American colleges and universities and provides policy recommendations for faculty and administrators who are involved in the leadership of their respective institutions. Knowing the key elements of such issues as artistic expression, political correctness, academic freedom in church-related colleges and universities, and subpoenaed research information and protected sources and being able to integrate an understanding of the legal implications of academic freedom as defined and interpreted by the AAUP empowers campus leaders to make informed decisions with serious implications for faculty academic freedom.

Challenges to academic freedom will not fade away. Colleges and universities must stand ready to act with speed and certainty when the intellectual liberty of faculty or students is challenged by individuals or groups who would restrict it unnecessarily from within or outside the campus. Institutional policies and procedures must be clear and evaluated regularly to ensure that faculty understand what freedoms and restrictions exist in their daily activities as scholars, teachers, and citizens, and so that the general public also might understand the values and responsibilities inherent in the academic enterprise.

DEFINING ACADEMIC FREEDOM

Academic freedom is a term used frequently in American higher education to describe the intellectual liberties required to explore, expound, and further knowledge. To understand the way academic freedom is defined and interpreted in the United States, it is necessary to review its conceptual evolution through history and modern times.

The Historical Emergence of Academic Freedom

It has been noted that "academic freedom is a modern term for an ancient idea" (Hofstadter and Metzger 1955, p. 3). The desire to question, debate, research, and record findings or opinion is recognized easily in the surviving record of ancient and medieval times. Plato's Academy, alive with the recorded dialogues of Socrates, was dedicated to the art of critical debate, the posing of questions, and the search for solutions. The ancient academy was not so much a location or structure but a community of thinkers drawn together in the logical quest for truth.

The gathering of scholars to record and investigate knowledge again surfaces in the medieval period. Like blacksmiths, carpenters, masons, and other craftsmen, scholars formed their own identity as members of a distinguishable trade. In the Middle Ages, the word "universitas" meant a collection of individuals organized as a body (Eby and Arrowood 1940).

The earliest discernable universities, those of Bologna, Paris, and later Oxford and Cambridge, were communities established by scholars where the learned lived, dined, and conversed with one another. Within these communities, a form of intellectual freedom existed that drew upon the strength of formally organized scholars.

Medieval professors had opportunities to explore and contribute to new realms of knowledge as long as they did not trespass on the doctrinal authority of the church. For the medieval professor, ". . . freedom was general, save in philosophy and theology. In law, in medicine, in grammar and mathematics, men were normally free to lecture and dispute as they would" (Haskins 1957, p. 52).

Though restricted by the religious beliefs and codes of those in authority, the faculty of the Middle Ages exerted considerable power in the selection of institutional leaders, the establishment of the institution's mission, the content of the curriculum, and the definition of academic standards. The medieval masters thereby set a foundation for the modern conception of faculty academic freedom (Olswang and Lee 1984).

The translation of the ancient and medieval English university to the eastern shore of 17th century North America was accomplished with considerable success. In establishing a college, the inhabitants of Massachusetts drew upon that with which they were familiar and comfortable: the English university. For example, the founding statutes of Harvard College were derived mainly from the Elizabethan statutes of Cambridge University (Brubacher and Rudy 1976; Hofstadter and Smith 1961). The Harvard College statutes, consonant with the values of the recently settled New England Puritans, focused heavily on knowing and honoring God through vigorous study and virtuous living. Recognizing the stark differences in the establishment of colleges in the colonies versus ancient and medieval Europe is important to understanding the evolution and development of academic freedom in the United States.

The trauma and reality of colonial settlements must be borne in mind when studying the structure of higher education and the role and function of faculty in America. While English settlers were beneficiaries of knowledge received at Oxford and Cambridge—institutions that existed well before English settlement in America—the stark eastern shores of North America contained no institutions of higher learning. The immediacy of settlement separated the American experience from that of Europe. As Hofstadter and Smith observe:

> *The European universities had been founded by groups of mature scholars; the American colleges were founded by their communities; and since they [American colleges] did not soon develop the mature scholars possessed from the beginning by their European predecessors but were staffed instead for generations mainly by young and transient tutors, the community leaders were reluctant to drop their reins of control* (Hofstadter and Smith 1961, vol. 1, p. 3).

Newly founded communities in America required a form and structure of higher learning that was sensitive to the perceived needs of their members and the perpetuation of core beliefs. The charters of Harvard College and the College of William and Mary reflect community values and interests rather than those of scholars drawn together voluntarily over time. The community interest lay in a literate populace that could serve God and the community effectively.

Community interests influenced heavily the form of governance that emerged in colleges in America. While the president and faculty (Fellows) at Harvard were considered a "corporation" implying some continuation of the English form of faculty governance, there also was created a board of "Overseers" comprising six magistrates and six ministers who actually governed the college (Hofstadter and Metzger 1955; Hofstadter and Smith 1961). This uneasy structure of governance was duplicated—albeit not precisely—at the College of William and Mary in Virginia. It was the beginning of lay government in higher education (Hofstadter and Metzger 1955).

The faculty of these emerging colleges were not free to select the president of the institution nor the curricula they taught. Early presidents of Harvard were selected by the Overseers and not by the faculty, who were isolated from the community which established the college for its own perpetuation. Faculty were not the sole or even the primary holders of power. Such power was now vested in the hands of a lay board.

These changes in college governance in America are significant to the history of academic freedom. External lay authority rather than internal corporate authority among scholars generated early debate about the role of higher learning and the purpose of faculty. Early in the 18th century, the question arose as to whether the purpose of higher learning was to indoctrinate students in the community's religious beliefs or to expose young men to varieties of learned opinion (See, for example, William Livingston's opposition to a sectarian college for New York [1753] in Hofstadter and Smith 1961, vol. 1, pp. 99-103).

The "Great Awakening" generated significant religious revival in America during the mid-18th century and further influenced the rise of denominational colleges where faculty allegiance to a particular sect was expected if not demanded. Faculty freedom was subjugated by religious fervor and denominational mores aimed at perpetuating a particular set of beliefs rather than knowledge alone.

The first decades of the 19th century brought the establishment of numerous colleges founded under Protestant and Catholic leadership. In antebellum America, there were at least 49 Presbyterian-related institutions in addition to 34 Methodist, 25 Baptist, 21 Congregationalist, 14 Roman Catholic, 11 Episcopalian, and six Lutheran colleges (Tewksbury 1932). Generally, these institutions were characterized by the restriction of faculty freedoms and an absence of intellectual vigor.

The era of "the old-time college," spanning the period between 1800 and 1860, is labeled by some historians as the "great retrogression" (Hofstadter and Metzger 1955). They interpret the backward movement of American higher education during this period as caused by the "epidemic of revivals, the rise of fundamentalism, and the all but unchecked ragings of the denominational spirit" (Hofstadter and Metzger 1955). Thus, at Princeton, a "progressive" president like Samuel Stanhope Smith could not create curricular change nor implement educational reforms in the early years of the 19th century, as the Presbyterian trustees of the institution reportedly cared more about stemming the rising tide of Episcopalianism than in improving Princeton's educational quality (Hofstadter and Metzger 1955).

As the 19th century progressed, denominational fervor in colleges was displaced by rising interest in the practical application of knowledge—due, in part, to the industrial revolution. Americans formed universities wherein science and research were to become a valued part of the academic enterprise. The emergence of universities in the United States occurred gradually and, in part, through the rise of professionally trained faculty who studied in Europe. Those who studied in German universities experienced the intellectual freedom available to students and faculty alike. Once the rewards of intellectual freedom were experienced abroad, they were not easily forgotten at home.

Some scholars contend that academic freedom was brought to the United States by professors trained in German universities (Veysey 1965). While this point is debatable, it is certain that German conceptions of academic freedom played a major role in framing modern notions of academic freedom in the United States.

It is significant that 19th century German universities recognized both the freedom of students ("Lernfreiheit") and professors ("Lehrfreiheit"). Lernfreiheit meant the absence of "coercions" in learning situations and the right of students to explore freely within academic disciplines (Hofstadter and Metzger 1955, p. 386). Lehrfreiheit meant professorial freedom to research and present findings through publication or instruction. Such dual recognition of intellectual freedom underscored the fact that Germans viewed their universities as places defined by free inquiry. According to Hofstadter and Metzger:

> *This freedom was not, as the Germans conceived it, an inalienable endowment of all men, nor was it a superadded attraction of certain universities and not of others; rather it was the distinctive prerogative of the academic profession, and the esssential condition of all universities. Without it, no institution had the right to call itself a 'university'* (1955, p. 387).

In the German university, students were free from the potentially harmful pressures of faculty or other persons of possible authority, and faculty enjoyed similar freedom. Academic freedom was a precondition for university status in Germany. There, the word "university" retained its medieval meaning of a corporate body of scholars. German faculty elected their academic officials, appointed lecturers, and nominated professors (Hofstadter and Metzger 1955).

German universities had no complex structures of administration; there were no university presidents, and the respective faculties were under deans that they elected. Numerous American academicians who returned home with graduate degrees from German institutions witnessed the corporate power of the faculty and the environment of freedom for those who participated in university education. These scholars helped to propel colleges in the United States into a new era.

The changing character of the United States in the later decades of the 19th century helped to achieve the written documentation of faculty freedoms. Postbellum America was in many ways far different than the country that existed prior to the Civil War. Out of the ashes and confusion of Reconstruction grew a need for order and stability. Industrialism and new forms of capitalism generated urban growth, dismantling old forms of the workplace and the community (Wiebe 1967). Laborers organized in the face of monolithic business and industry that left them with little sense of security or control.

The quest for definition of purpose and place in the midst of uncertainty was not lost on American academics. "From the late 19th century on, the definition of academic freedom underwent a series of changes, many of which reflected the relative insecurity of the academic profession as well as the cultural climate of the day" (Schrecker 1986, p. 14). Many faculty believed it necessary to formally document the standards that would govern, if not create, their "profession." Formal statements on academic freedom were developed by the organization of the AAUP.

Popular Notions of Academic Freedom

"Popular" is used to denote that which is prevalent either in printed form or general understanding. As scholars debated the definition of academic freedom in the late 19th and early 20th centuries, their writing reflected the values of democratic society to bolster their case for free, responsible inquiry. Early academic freedom definitions appealed to notions of basic human or constitutional rights. "Academic freedom often became a symbol of independence from onerous authority" in the early 20th century (Veysey 1965, p. 397).

The association of academic freedom with basic human freedoms in a democratic society was accomplished in part by well-publicized confrontations between faculty and university authorities. The dismissals of Richard T. Ely, a University of Wisconsin economist, for advocating the use of strikes and boycotts; Edward W. Bemis, an economist at the University of Chicago, for his comments against the railroads; and Edward A. Ross, a Stanford University sociologist, for expressed opposition to the use of cheap, unskilled oriental labor in the construction of railroads, are examples of publicized cases that demonstrated the loss of employment at the expense of exercising free expression (See Rudolph 1962).

These cases and others were known to those who gathered together to document American academic freedom. In developing parameters for academic freedom, American scholars went beyond the German model of Lehrfreiheit to examine faculty freedoms both within and outside of the academy. They thereby formed a link between academic freedom and the freedoms enjoyed by other citizens. Questions concerning freedom of expression within the classroom were joined with questions pertaining to speech outside of the college or university.

Prominent among the three freedoms included in the AAUP's 1915 General Declaration of Principles was freedom of "extra-mural utterance and action" (Hofstadter and Smith 1961, vol. 2, p. 861). This freedom, and the absence of discussion on student academic freedom, was a significant departure from the German construction of academic freedom. According to the 1915 principles, teachers were to practice self-restraint in making extramural statements but also were to enjoy the "political rights vouchsafed to every citizen" (Hofstadter and Smith 1961, vol. 2, p. 874). While incompetence and "moral delinquency" were considered legitimate grounds for faculty dismissal, the 1915 declaration asserted that faculty should be guaranteed ". . . absolute freedom of thought, of inquiry, of discussion and of teaching . . ." (Hofstadter and Smith 1961, vol. 2, p. 875). The declaration moved delicately between a discussion of freedoms held commonly by all Americans—scholars and non-scholars alike—to those necessary for unfettered academic inquiry. Civil liberty was used to empower, if not beget, academic freedom.

The 1915 declaration held that responsible governance was necessary to protect the public trust in having institutions of higher learning free from the domination of "propaganda" that expressed the values or interests of an individual or organization. The declaration maintained that the trustees of public institutions were ". . . trustees for the public" and not for their individual interests (Hofstadter and Smith 1961, vol. 2, p. 863). According to the authors,

Trustees of such universities (that appeal for public support) have no moral right to bind the reason or conscience of any professor. All claim to such right is waived by the appeal to the general public for contributions and for moral support in the maintenance, not of propaganda, but of a non-partisan institution of learning (Hofstadter and Smith 1961, vol. 2, p. 863).

Moreover, the early members of the AAUP believed that, while a university teacher

. . . accepts a responsibility to the authorities of the instition in which he serves, in the essentials of his professional activity his duty is to the wider public to which the institution itself is morally amenable (Hofstadter and Smith 1961, vol. 2, p. 866).

The declaration attempted to tie the function of the university and faculty to the interests of society at large, contributing to the formation of an early definition and popular notion of academic freedom.

The 1915 declaration marks an important beginning for the written documentation of academic freedom and development of a collective identity in the United States. Frederick Rudolph noted that the establishment of the AAUP in 1915 ". . . symbolized the arrival of academic man in America" (1962, p. 415). However, the two and a half decades following the 1915 declaration were critical to the development of perhaps the most widely known and endorsed statement of academic freedom in the United States: the AAUP's 1940 Statement of Principles and Interpretive Comments on Academic Freedom and Tenure.

AAUP's 1940 Statement on Academic Freedom

During the early 20th century, the emerging American academic community was divided sharply over the meaning and purpose of academic freedom. The college presidents who formed the AAC in 1915 rejected the AAUP's 1915 Declaration of Principles as unacceptable on a number of counts. Hofstadter and Metzger suggest that the AAC may have been annoyed by the exclusion of presidents and faculty beneath the rank of full professor from AAUP membership. Moreover, the presidents were suspicious of the role and purpose of academic tenure as put forth in the AAUP's 1915 Declaration of Principles (1955).

Despite disagreements, the AAC's Academic Freedom Commission's 1922 report on academic freedom acknowledged the work of the AAUP and agreed with the major elements of the AAUP's definition. The commission supported several ideas including: 1) teachers should have freedom to teach as long as they retained neutrality and were professionally competent (Hofstadter and Metzger 1955); 2) faculty should be able to excercise extramural freedom to the degree that they did not damage or injure the name or reputation of their institutions; and 3) faculty appointments and the termination contracts were most appropriately done with the input of the relevant academic departments.

The AAC and the AAUP moved closer together in their conceptual and pragmatic views of academic freedom. In the aftermath of a series of joint conferences initiated in 1934, the two organizations agreed upon what is known now as the 1940 Statement of Principles on Academic Freedom and Tenure (AAUP 1990). The fact that two of the early higher education associations—comprising presidents and faculty—united to define and interpret the meaning and parameters of academic freedom contributed to making the 1940 Statement the centerpiece of popular notions of academic freedom in the United States.

The purpose of the 1940 Statement was to ". . . promote public understanding and support of academic freedom and tenure and agreement upon procedures to assure them in colleges and universities" (AAUP 1990, p. 3). In the first few lines of the 1940 Statement, the representatives of the AAUP and AAC appealed to the public for a common understanding of and support for academic freedom and tenure and the due-process procedures deemed necessary to undergird these principles. The authors underscored that the common good is dependent upon intellectual freedom. While this line of reasoning is not pursued in detail within the 1940 Statement, it fits well with popular notions of freedom and democracy.

The 1940 Statement identifies four basic academic freedoms to which college and university teachers are entitled: the freedom to research, to publish the results of such research, to teach, and to communicate extramurally. Each freedom has attendant responsibilities. "Full freedom in research and in the publication of the results" is dependent upon the teacher's "adequate performance" in other areas of academic responsibility (AAUP 1990, p. 3). Moreover, the authors of the 1940 Statement recommended that research done for pay "be based upon an understanding with the authorities of the institution" (AAUP 1990, p. 3).

The freedom to teach in the classroom focuses on teaching within the faculty member's subject area. The 1940 Statement recommends that faculty resist introducing "controversial matter" in the classroom having no relationship to their teaching area. The AAUP's 1970 Interpretive Comments on this matter indicate that the purpose of the 1940 Statement is not to suppress discussion of the controversial in classroom settings but to urge that instruction be centered on the subject matter of the class (AAUP 1990).

Framers of the 1940 Statement noted that limitations on faculty academic freedom arising from the religious orientation or other "aims" of the college or university should be

The 1940 Statement identifies . . . the freedom to research, to publish the results of such research, to teach, and to communicate extramurally.

put in writing at the time a faculty appointment is made (AAUP 1990). While this provision is included in the paragraph pertaining to classroom teaching, the AAUP views the provision as applying to all elements of faculty academic freedom. The 1970 Interpretive Comments state that "most church-related institutions no longer need or desire the departure from the principle of academic freedom implied in the 1940 Statement, and we do not now endorse such a departure" (AAUP 1990, p. 6).

In addressing the academic freedom of faculty outside of the college or university setting, the AAUP 1940 Statement reminds that faculty are citizens, members of a profession, and officers of their college or university (AAUP 1990). The role of teachers in these communities carries overlapping responsibilities. The 1940 Statement indicates that when faculty members "speak or write as citizens, they should be free from institutional censorship or discipline, but their special position in the community imposes special obligations" (AAUP 1990, p. 4).

Even when speaking extramurally, faculty have a responsibility to uphold the reputation of their profession and institutions. In upholding this responsibility, college and university faculty are to be accurate, careful in their communication, tolerant of the views of others, and assiduous in their efforts to make known that they are not speaking on behalf of their institution.

The 1940 Statement of Principles and Interpretive Comments on Academic Freedom and Tenure is at the center of popular notions of academic freedom in the United States. Not only is the statement officially endorsed by more than 140 professional organizations, but it serves an important function in the legal system as well, where the courts are hesitant to provide their own interpretation of academic freedom. AAUP professional standards sometimes are invoked legally to ". . . express academic custom generally . . ." (AAUP 1990, p. x). The use of the statement as a reference in legal cases is perhaps the most telling evidence that the 1940 Statement has attained the status of being the most common notion of academic freedom in the United States.

Summary
Academic freedom is not a modern concept but is rooted in the ancient record of scholarship. In America, academic free-

dom emerged with the rise of universities that were patterned largely after those found in Germany, which stressed scientific research and open inquiry. In the opening decades of the 20th century, American scholars defined academic freedom to provide the basic principles for free inquiry in the United States.

By mid-century, university professors and presidents combined their efforts through the AAUP and the AAC to create the 1940 Statement of Principles and Interpretive Comments on Academic Freedom and Tenure. The 1940 Statement documented in writing the meaning of academic freedom, and through its subsequent recognition by numerous professional associations, societies, and American courts, has become the popular notion of academic freedom in the United States. Those freedoms documented in the 1940 Statement include the freedom to teach, research, publish, and to speak extramurally.

THE LEGAL ASPECTS OF THE AAUP 1940 STATEMENT OF PRINCIPLES ON ACADEMIC FREEDOM AND TENURE

The legal aspect of academic freedom in American colleges and universities is an exceptionally complex topic. The complexity is rooted, in part, in five elements: the intricacies of constitutional law, the broad sweep of the academic freedom categories found within the AAUP's 1940 Statement of Principles on Academic Freedom and Tenure, differences between public and independent institutions, differences between tenured and non-tenured faculty, and the historical development of voluminous federal and state case law which relates to professorial academic freedom.

This section attempts to manage some of these complexities by using the AAUP 1940 Statement of Principles on Academic Freedom and Tenure as the major organizational unit. Specifically, the law—especially constitutional law—is examined within the scope of the freedom of professors to conduct research and publish, teach in the classroom, and speak or communicate as citizens. Much of the law as it relates to academic freedom is based upon constitutional rights and particularly First Amendment protections of free speech. However, constitutional protections generally apply only to public colleges and universities and not to independent institutions. It is important, therefore, to differentiate between public and independent colleges and universities when discussing higher education and the law.

As state-supported institutions, public colleges and universities and their faculty are under the purview of constitutional law. Independent colleges and universities are private entities which are neither created by the state nor maintained through public funding. Independent institutions and their faculty are not, therefore, under the purview of the Constitution. Faculty in independent colleges and universities primarily must rely upon contractual law for protection of academic freedom.

These legal differences have substantial implications for academic freedom. For example, the on-campus speech of public college and university faculty is protected largely by the Constitution, whereas the speech of independent college faculty is not. Section four examines in greater detail the legal dimension of academic freedom within church-related colleges and universities.

Not only does the public or non-public status of an institution affect the legalities of a faculty's academic freedom, but also the tenured or non-tenured status of each individual faculty member as well. Tenured faculty have a property-right investment in their employment and as a result are accorded certain due-process rights under the 14th Amendment. While non-tenured faculty do not have property rights and associated due-process protections, in theory they cannot be fired legally for constitutionally protected freedoms, although in practical terms they are vulnerable. If, for example, a non-tenured faculty member criticizes the administration and his or her contract is not renewed, there are no grounds for redress unless he or she can prove the critical speech is the reason behind the actions of the administration.

Before turning to the legal aspects of academic freedom as it relates to the various AAUP components, it is important first to review briefly the U.S. Supreme Court's treatment of academic freedom over the last half century and whether the court has embraced the concept in a manner that accords it constitutional status.

Academic Freedom and the Supreme Court

Scholars have debated for decades whether academic freedom is protected by the Constitution (Boudin 1983; Herberg 1971; Katz 1983; Matherne 1984; Murphy 1961; O'Neil 1984; Pritchett 1971; Van Alstyne 1972; Yudof 1987). As a term, academic freedom does not expressly appear in the language of the Constitution but, as will be seen in the following, the term is recognized and used by the Supreme Court. The various freedoms included in the AAUP 1940 Statement of Principles on Academic Freedom relate directly to constitutional protections, such as a professor's First Amendment right to speak as a citizen.

The Supreme Court's belief that academic freedom is a valuable element of American society and one worthy of federal protection spans decades. Several of the cases where the justices of the court wrote eloquently and at length on the importance of academic freedom involved the imposition of state loyalty oaths or the forced disclosure of organizations to which faculty belonged. These cases are valuable not only for the constitutional protections and legal precedent that they established but also for the fertile discussion that the court provided recognizing the value and contributions of academic freedom within American society.

In this brief review, cases were selected to provide an introduction to the way in which the Supreme Court views the intersection of academic freedom with civil rights protected by the Constitution. While not all of the academic freedom-related cases decided by the Supreme Court are included, these major cases illustrate academic freedom as interpreted by the court, its valued status, and its relationship to the Constitution.

The Supreme Court held in a number of cases that government may not intrude into the academic life of a college, university, or faculty member without reasons that are urgent and compelling. In *Sweezy v. New Hampshire*, 354 U.S. 234 (1957), the court held that the University of New Hampshire denied a faculty member named Paul Sweezy due process of law under the 14th Amendment after he was held in contempt of court for refusing to answer questions concerning the contents of one of his lectures and his knowledge of the Progressive Party of the State and its members. The majority court opinion considered only the question of whether Sweezy's due-process rights were violated. It did not consider Sweezy's First Amendment claims which involved protecting such matters as the content of his speech within the classroom (See Van Alstyne 1990, p. 110). However, the court did provide a defense of academic freedom and its importance to civilization. In his opinion, Chief Justice Warren wrote,

> *The essentiality of freedom in the community of American universities is almost self-evident. No one should underestimate the vital role in a democracy that is played by those who guide and train our youth. To impose any straitjacket upon the intellectual leaders in our colleges and universities would imperil the future of our Nation. No field of education is so thoroughly comprehended by man that new discoveries cannot yet be made. Particularly is that true in the social sciences, where few, if any, principles are accepted as absolutes. Scholarship cannot flourish in an atmosphere of suspicion and distrust. Teachers and students must always remain free to inquire, to study and to evaluate, to gain new maturity and understanding; otherwise our civilization will stagnate and die (Sweezy 1957, p. 250).*

Warren's comments regarding the compelling need for freedom within higher education institutions were not core to the disposition of the case, which hinged on *due-process rights* and not on the question of professorial academic freedom. That Chief Justice Warren wove into his opinion the term and notion of academic freedom and its importance to civilization and the progression of knowledge is indicative of the recognition of such freedom and its value by the Supreme Court.

However, it is through Justice Frankfurter's concurring opinion that one sees not only the clear acknowledged value of academic freedom but also recognition of the linkage of academic freedom to the First Amendment and the need to protect it from unnecessary governmental intrusion. Frankfurter set forth a compelling defense of academic freedom by focusing on the endangerment of First Amendment rights via governmental inquiries into the content of Sweezy's lecture at the University of New Hampshire. By connecting academic freedom to the First Amendment through Sweezy's speech (or lecture), Frankfurter proved able to juxtapose the interest of the state in examining the content of Sweezy's lecture with the interest of protecting free speech as exercised within an academic environment.

According to Frankfurter, "when weighed against the grave harm resulting from governmental intrusion into the intellectual life of a university, such justification for compelling a witness to discuss the contents of his lecture appears grossly inadequate" (*Sweezy*, p. 261). Frankfurter asserted further that "political power must abstain from intrusion into this activity of [intellectual] freedom, pursued in the interest of wise government and the people's well-being, except for reasons that are exigent and obviously compelling" (p. 262).

As will be seen in additional detail later in this section, Justice Frankfurter provided a significant defense of academic freedom within the classroom in addition to academic freedom in general. Frankfurter held that the First Amendment protected Sweezy in his refusal to disclose the content of his lecture at the University of New Hampshire (Van Alstyne 1990). In so doing, Frankfurter linked academic freedom with the First Amendment.

In *Sweezy*, the Supreme Court recognized that governmental intrusion into the academic life of a college or university, absent an unusually compelling need, would result in an environment of fear and suspicion necessarily leading to the suppression of intellectual inquiry and freedom of expression. This same recognition is evident in *Keyishian v. Board of*

Regents, 365 U.S. 589 (1967), wherein the Supreme Court carried forward its linkage of academic freedom with constitutional protections.

The facts surrounding *Keyishian* involved the imposition of teacher loyalty laws and regulations in the state of New York, which required faculty members to sign a certificate indicating that they were not Communists, and that they would inform the university president if they had been members of the Communist party at some previous juncture. Failure to comply with this requirement resulted in termination of employment. When Keyishian, an instructor in English at the University of New York, refused to sign the certificate, his one-year-term contract was not renewed. Keyishian and others subsequently brought suit contending that sections of the New York Education Law were unconstitutionally vague.

For example, one section required removal of teachers for "treasonable or seditious" utterances or acts (*Keyishian* 1967). The problem with the New York law was that " . . . no teacher can know just where the line is drawn between 'seditious' and non-seditious utterances and acts" (p. 599). The vagueness of the law and the attendant danger of unknowingly committing a criminal act under the law constricted free speech. As Brennan stated, "It would be a bold teacher who would not stay as far as possible from utterances or acts which might jeopardize his living by enmeshing him in this intricate machinery [of administrative enforcement of the law]" (p. 601).

While recognizing that New York had a legitimate interest in trying to protect its system of education from subversive activity, the opinion of the court stated clearly that even a legitimate and substantial governmental purpose cannot suppress civil liberties such as freedom of expression when a more narrow means of achieving the government's purpose could be employed (See also *Shelton v. Tucker*, 364 U.S. 479 [1960]).

As in Frankfurter's opinion in *Sweezy*, the court in *Keyishian* was cognizant of the fact that the interests of the state must be weighed against the protection of free expression. However, in *Keyishian*, the majority opinion of the court specifically linked academic freedom to the First Amendment. In one of the most strongly worded defenses of academic freedom, the court noted,

> *Our Nation is deeply committed to safeguarding academic freedom, which is of transcendent value to all of us and*

not merely to the teachers concerned. That freedom is there-
fore a special concern of the First Amendment, which does
not tolerate laws that cast a pall of orthodoxy over the class-
room (p. 603).

The court underscored the important constitutional principle
that government regulations that bear upon First Amendment
freedoms must be tailored narrowly so as not to unnecessarily
impinge upon or suppress such freedoms. By linking this principle to academic freedom, the court caused the relationship
between the First Amendment and academic freedom to grow
tighter.

The Supreme Court not only related academic freedom to
constitutional protections but also has defended in its opinions the rights of faculty and higher education institutions
in general to make decisions based upon academic judgment.
Two major Supreme Court decisions demonstrate this defense
of institutional and professorial academic freedom to make
academic-related judgments: *University of California Regents*
v. Bakke, 438 U.S. 265 (1978), and *Regents of the University*
of Michigan v. Ewing, 474 U.S. 214 (1985).

At first glance, *Bakke* appears to have little to do with the
Supreme Court's view or interpretation of academic freedom.
While the major issue in the case was whether the dual-track
admissions programs at the University of California at Davis'
Medical School violated the Equal Protection Clause of the
14th Amendment, the case provided an opportunity for Justice
Powell to further interpret the meaning and purpose of academic freedom in higher education. Although in delivering
the opinion of the court, Powell held that the special admissions program for minority students at the UC-Davis Medical
School violated the Equal Protection Clause, he recognized
in his own opinion that it is constitutionally permissible—
and in the interest of academic freedom—for a university to
strive for a diverse student body.

Powell wrote that a diverse student body contributed to
the exchange and interplay of ideas and opinions that are
essential to higher education and academic freedom. He
noted that the University of California Regents,

. . . in arguing that its universities must be accorded the
right to select those students who will contribute the most
to the robust exchange of ideas, . . . invokes a countervailing

constitutional interest, that of the First Amendment. In this light, the petitioner (the University of California) must be viewed as seeking to achieve a goal that is of paramount importance to the fulfillment of its mission (p. 313).

Powell argued that the university had a constitutional right to pursue racial diversity as one goal of its admissions policy as it related justifiably to the enrichment of the intellectual exchange that is supposed to take place within an institution of higher learning. His defense of educational diversity was an acknowledgment and defense of the academic freedom of an institution.

As Powell recognized, academic freedom has as one of its major purposes the free exchange of different opinions and exposure to different "mores" (*Bakke* 1978, p. 313). This recognition of the right of institutions to set admissions criteria within educational parameters demonstrated not only Powell's respect for the purpose of academic freedom but also respect for the competence of college and university leaders to make academic decisions. This is recognized also in *Regents of the University of Michigan v. Ewing*, 474 U.S. 214 (1985).

In *Ewing*, the court considered whether the University of Michigan deprived a student named Ewing of property without due process after it refused to allow him to retake a test administered by the National Board of Medical Examiners (NBME) and dropped him from the academic program in which he was enrolled. Ewing's academic performance in the university's "Inteflex" program (a special six-year program of study) was poor, and his score on the NBME Part I test was the lowest ever made by an Inteflex student. As part of his complaint, Ewing asserted that he had a property interest in his continued enrollment in the Inteflex program and that in dismissing him, the university acted in an "arbitrary" and "capricious" manner and violated his substantive due-process rights. While the Court of Appeals for the sixth circuit agreed with Ewing, the Supreme Court did not.

The court's opinion provided an opportunity to demonstrate its respect for faculty expertise in making decisions regarding academic matters. Writing for the court, Justice Stevens asserted that

When judges are asked to review the substance of a genuinely academic decision, such as this one, they should

As Powell recognized, academic freedom has as one of its major purposes the free exchange of different opinions and exposure to different "mores."

show great respect for the faculty's professional judgment. Plainly, they may not override it unless it is such a substantial departure from accepted academic norms as to demonstrate that the person or committee responsible did not actually exercise professional judgment (p. 225).

The court's opinion defends strongly the professional judgment of faculty. It states "plainly" that such judgment may not be pushed aside by the courts unless there is some major movement away from such professional judgment.

This brief review of Supreme Court cases as they pertain to academic freedom indicates that:

- The Supreme Court recognizes academic freedom as a "special concern" of the First Amendment (*Keyishian* 1967, p. 603).
- Government may not intrude into the academic life of colleges and universities unless there is an unusually compelling need to do so and, even then, the interest of the state must be weighed against the need to protect free expression.
- The most narrow means of protecting the interest of the state must be used so as to not unnecessarily suppress free speech.
- The Supreme Court maintains a deep respect for the professional judgment of colleges and universities and their faculty in academic matters.

The remainder of this section is dedicated to a review of the law as it relates to the academic freedom components contained in the AAUP's 1940 Statement.

Freedom in Research and in the Publication of Results
The AAUP *Policy Documents and Reports* contains a number of references to professorial freedoms and responsibilities in research. According to the 1940 Statement, "teachers are entitled to full freedom in research and in the publication of results, subject to the adequate performance of their other academic duties; but research for pecuniary return should be based upon an understanding with the authorities of the institution" (AAUP 1990, p. 3). Moreover, the *Policy Documents and Reports* contain two other statements which pertain in whole or in part to research.

The "Statement on Professional Ethics" indicates that "although professors may follow subsidiary interests, these interests must never seriously hamper or compromise freedom of inquiry" (AAUP 1990, p. 76). The statement "On Preventing Conflicts of Interest in Government-Sponsored Research at Universities" (AAUP 1990, pp. 83-85) addresses the need for standards which provide some measure of protection against conflicts of interest in government-sponsored research. Collectively, these statements indicate that professors should be free to pursue and share knowledge provided they fulfill their other academic responsibilities; should formulate policies with their institutions in cases where payment is received for conducting research; and should not engage in pursuits which limit significantly free inquiry or produce conflicts of interest.

The statements reflect a shift in the perceived source of threats to professorial freedoms to research and publish posed by American society since the 1940 Statement was adopted. Broadly stated, concerns regarding external (or non-institutionally based) restrictions are outpacing concerns of internal threats as faculty increasingly become involved in sponsored research activities (See Eisenberg 1988). Moreover, externally based threats to freedom to conduct research are multiplying with the increasing number of researchers subpoenaed to testify and/or provide research data as part of legal investigations.

The issue of compelled disclosure, or the relinquishment of research sources, research content, or testimony via subpoena, is only one aspect of the freedom to research and publish. Other issues include such diverse topics as sponsored research, animal rights, and fetal tissue research, and each has its own unique set of applicable cases. It is nearly impossible to find common Supreme Court threads regarding such uncommon subjects, and it is impossible within the scope of this report to explore each one. Therefore, for purposes of discussion and reasonable limitations, compelled disclosure is used as a vehicle to examine the legal aspects of academic research since this issue is impacting heavily the academic world. Section four addresses the sponsored research issue and returns to compelled disclosure to address some more practical aspects of the topic.

Compelled disclosure

The legal aspects surrounding the freedom of research in general are complex given the varieties of issues involved, differences in state regulations, and the myriad of federal rules and regulations that apply to research-related issues and cases. This complexity extends also to the issue of compelled testimony or the relinquishment of research material by subpoena.

The compelled disclosure scenario involves two parties engaged in litigation. The academic researcher is not a party to the suit and has no legal interest in its outcome. One or both parties seek to get the professor's research results, and the professor refuses the subpoena. The subpoena may require the researcher to appear in court and testify, and/or it may request raw data or notes, compelling disclosure of the researcher's findings and/or opinions. The researcher's limited choice of poor responses includes being held in contempt of court or filing suit against the subpoenaing party.

There is no consensus among the courts as to the handling of a researcher's refusal to comply with a subpoena. However, two major approaches may be taken by courts to analyze cases or taken by researchers' attorneys to prepare a defense. The approaches are 1) constitutionally based and 2) non-constitutionally based.

The constitutional approach to refusing compelled disclosure via subpoena can be based upon First or 14th Amendment claims. Among the many approaches to seeking constitutional shields, the researcher might claim a First Amendment right to academic freedom (as established by *Sweezy* and *Keyishian*) or claim a journalist's First Amendment right to protect confidential sources.

In the first instance, the researcher can invoke constitutional considerations by declaring that such disclosure is a violation of his academic freedom (O'Neil 1983; Matherne 1984). Such claims are rarely—if ever—successful. It is noted that " . . . parties often use the academic freedom argument to add a constitutional aura to an otherwise bland contractual dispute" in an attempt to raise the judicial stakes (Matherne 1984, p. 186). However,

> *Even in the cases in which courts seriously consider an academic freedom claim, (it's just) . . . one factor in a balancing test. . . . Furthermore, courts recognize that the concerns*

*which academic freedom allegedly protects fall under other
more specific constitutional guarantees like freedom of
expression, freedom of religion, due process, or the rule
against vagueness. The academic researcher, therefore,
should not rely solely on an academic freedom claim to
frustrate an order to disclose his research* (Matherne 1984,
p. 615).

That researchers should not place total reliance on academic
freedom claims to protect themselves from court-mandated
disclosure is evidenced in two cases involving the disclosure
of tenure decisions. In re: *Dinnan*, 661 F.2d 426 (5th Cir.
1981), and *Gray v. Board of Higher Education*, 92 F.R.D. 87,
90 (S.D.N.Y. 1981), rev'd, 692 F.2d 901 (2d Cir. 1982), faculty
members serving on tenure committees claimed an academic
freedom privilege in refusing to disclose votes on tenure
cases. In both cases the courts held that academic freedom—
even if considered a subset of the First Amendment—was not
alone a sufficient defense to prevent disclosure of the tenure
votes (Matherne 1984).

In addition to academic freedom, another possible tactic
to avoid compelled disclosure under the First Amendment
is to assert an analogy with the journalist's First Amendment
claim of protecting confidential sources. Of course, this tactic
is not advisable if the research subjects are monkeys or Jeeps.
Researchers who have data culled from personal interviews
or patient medical records may need to protect the anonymity
of their sources in much the same way as journalists. At times,
researchers promise confidentiality to research sources in
order to gain their participation. Moreover, maintaining confidentiality often is necessary to retain the researcher's cred-
ibility for future research endeavors on sensitive matters (See
Monaghan 1993).

While the Supreme Court ruled that journalists cannot
refuse on constitutional grounds to answer questions regarding sensitive sources posed by a grand jury (*Branzburg v.
Hayes*, 408 U.S. 665 [1972]), subsequent lower court litigation
made the *Branzburg* decision more the exception than the
rule. It is not uncommon "within certain limits now recognized in our law" for journalists to prevail in protecting their
sources from disclosure under the First Amendment (O'Neil
1983).

The Supreme Court recognized in *Branzburg* that "the

informative function asserted by representatives of the organized press . . . is also performed . . . by academic researchers . . . " for some researchers outwardly claim the same rights as members of the press in maintaining the confidentiality of their sources (See Monaghan 1993). However, the question still remains as to the extent that the journalist's claim to confidential sources extends to academic researchers. Researchers also can claim confidential protection of sources without invoking the analogous journalist-source relationship. This will be discussed in greater detail in the non-constitutional response to compelled disclosure.

The second major constitutionally based response that can be employed in response to a subpoena involves 14th Amendment protection to liberty or property rights through the due-process clause. The researcher may claim his or her right to conduct research under the lofty umbrella of "liberty," an argument not established in court (Matherne 1984). Or, a researcher may claim property rights to his or her research.

To claim a 14th Amendment due-process violation of property rights, it is necessary for a scholar to establish a property interest in his or her research. Here it is important to note that "courts have held that an academic only has a property interest in research data before he publishes it" (Matherne 1984, p. 610). Once a researcher has published findings, the findings are in the public domain and the researcher's property interests are forfeited. Therefore, a researcher may prove able to claim a loss of property or liberty without due process of law if the researcher is subpoenaed and forced to provide information or data before it is shared through publication.

While constitutionally based resistance to forced disclosure of research rarely is successful, non-constitutionally based approaches to subpoenas are more effective and easier to adjudicate successfully (Matherne 1984). Non-constitutionally based approaches to subpoenas are based primarily upon procedural guidelines outlined in federal rules and attendant case law.

Under this approach, a "balancing test" is employed by the courts to weigh a plaintiff's interest in obtaining subpoenaed information versus the public interest in ensuring the confidentiality of an academic's research (Matherne 1984). In considering the subpoena of information, the courts basically evaluate 1) the relevance of the subpoenaed information to the legal consideration at hand; 2) whether the information can be obtained elsewhere; and 3) the burden that it imposes on the researcher, including the breadth of the request, the subpoenaed party's ability to incur expenses, the time period of the request, and the reasons underlying the request (Matherne 1984).

"In effect, the court is asked to balance the need for access to the research information against the burden that such access would impose on those who maintain the information. The decision to compel disclosure within this framework is based on the circumstances of the individual case and the characteristics of the individual research" (Cecil and Boruch 1988, p. 183).

Federal courts repeatedly use this non-constitutional balancing approach in addressing the enforcement of subpoenas seeking disclosure of academic research. In *Richards of Rockford, Inc. v. Pacific Gas and Electric Co.*, 71 F.R.D. 388 (N.D. Cal. 1976), the court determined that the subpoenaed information was not significant to the civil suit and could be obtained elsewhere. Further, the court recognized that the subpoena—if enforced—would destroy confidentiality and stifle research.

In a comparable finding, the 7th Circuit Court of Appeals used the balancing test to decide in *DOW Chemical Co. v. Allen*, 672 F.2d 1262 (7th Cir. 1982), that a researcher's burden of compliance outweighed the requesting party's need for the information sought. Moreover, the court recognized in *DOW* that such forced disclosure is "an intrusion into the university life which would risk substantially chilling the exercise of academic freedom" (*DOW*, p. 1,277).

The district court in *Wright v. Jeep Corp.*, 547 F. Supp. 871 (E.D. Mich. 1982), denied a motion to quash a subpoena for academic research but decided that the defendant and not the researcher had to pay for the cost of the documents subpoenaed and for the inconvenience (Matherne 1984). In deciding the case, the district court determined that no First Amendment privilege exists to protect the disclosure of academic research, and no common-law privilege protects academic research completely from disclosure. The court did recognize the burden involved in the transmittal of subpoenaed information and issued an order to make the burden reasonable.

Issues of confidentiality reappear in cases where non-constitutionally based resistance to the disclosure of research is involved. Federal rules can be invoked to consider and balance the researchers' need to keep sources confidential with the need for the disclosure of information. Also, researchers can claim the need to protect confidential sources under the common-law privilege codified under Rule 501 of the Federal Rules of Evidence (Matherne 1984). Generally, to claim a need to protect confidential sources the following requirements must be met:

1. The information must have been relayed in confidence;
2. Confidentiality must be essential to the relationship between parties;
3. The community at large must have an interest in fostering the confidential relationship; and
4. The injury resulting from the disclosure must be greater than the benefit of disclosure.

Moreover, for courts to determine if subpoenaed material is subject to common-law privilege it is necessary as a second step " . . . to balance the need for an evidentiary privilege against the countervailing need for full disclosure of all relevant facts" (Matherne 1988, p. 608). Courts are sensitive to the disclosure of confidential information, especially in instances where disclosing identities would seriously compromise the privacy of participants in research projects (See, for example, *Deitchman v. Squibb & Sons*, 740 F.2d 556 (7th Cir. 1984), and *Farnsworth v. Proctor and Gamble*, 104 F.R.D. 335 (N.D. Ga. 1984), aff'd, 758 F.2d 1545 (11th Cir. 1985).

Where possible, courts generally seek to require the names of research participants removed from subpoenaed information to protect confidentiality. "Courts have been quite resourceful in identifying interests that do cause them to deny disclosure or to settle on partial disclosure that will not disrupt research" (Monaghan 1993, p. A-10).

A brief discussion of cases pertaining to the freedom to research and publish reveals that:

• This complex topic gives rise to a vast array of diverse legal issues such as compelled disclosure, protection of confidential sources, and sponsored research.
• Faculty also incur attendant responsibilities to their institutions, their profession, their sources, and society to preserve academic integrity in the face of many issues.

- There is no court consensus regarding resistance to compelled disclosure of research, and results vary widely with each case.
- The issue of compelled disclosure perhaps is best examined using the non-constitutional balancing approach rather than constitutional approach.

Freedom in the Classroom

The 1940 Statement indicates that "teachers are entitled to freedom in the classroom in discussing their subject, but they should be careful not to introduce into their teaching controversial matter which has no relation to their subject" (AAUP 1990, p. 3). The AAUP and AAC's 1970 Interpretive Comments on this subject state that "the intent of this statement is not to discourage what is 'controversial.' Controversy is at the heart of free academic inquiry which the entire statement is designed to foster. The passage serves to underscore the need for teachers to avoid persistently intruding material which has no relation to their subject" (AAUP 1990, p. 6). The central concern of the 1940 Statement on freedom in the classroom is the freedom to discuss *relevant* subject matter, even when such subject matter is controversial. The onus of responsibility placed on teachers is to remain on the subject.

While the case law pertaining to freedom in the classroom is consistent with and supportive of the classroom freedoms articulated in the 1940 Statement and the 1970 Interpretive Comments, the courts have given colleges and universities a large degree of control over what takes place inside the classroom and on the campus.

Institutional rights

Federal courts recognize that government cannot impede upon the civil rights of faculty minus "exigent and obviously compelling" reasons (*Sweezy* 1957, p. 262). However, the courts recognize also the rights of colleges and universities to set and maintain pedagogical standards, see that appropriate course subject matter is taught by the faculty, and ensure that faculty are not engaged in the use of unprotected speech within the classroom. "The classroom is . . . the arena where institutional authority is greatest and courts are most hesitant to enter" (Kaplin 1985, p. 192. See also Katz 1983).

Federal court decisions hold that colleges and universities have the right to expect their faculty to use teaching methods that are appropriate to the institution wherein they teach (*Clark v. Holmes*, 474 F.2d 928 [7th Cir. 1972]; *Hetrick v. Martin*, 480 F.2d 705 [1973]) and to expect that institutional academic standards—including course content and grading standards—will be maintained (*Lovelace v. Southeastern Massachusetts University*, 793 F.2d 419 [1st Cir. 1986]).

Clark involved (among other issues) an untenured faculty member who, in the opinion of the Northern Illinois University, overemphasized sex in his health survey course. The 7th Circuit Court of Appeals found no First Amendment violation when the university decided, in part because of his tendency to depart from proper coverage of subject matter, not to rehire Clark. In its decision, the court stated that " . . . we do not conceive of academic freedom to be a license for uncontrolled expression at variance with established curricular contents and internally destructive of the proper functioning of the institution . . . " (p. 931).

One year after *Clark*, and in a comparable case, the 6th Circuit Court of Appeals ruled in *Hetrick v. Martin* that Eastern Kentucky University acted in a constitutionally permissible way when it terminated the employment of a non-tenured faculty member because her teaching methods and educational philosophy were incompatible with the university. The faculty member, Phyllis Hetrick, used statements such as "I am an unwed mother" (she was a divorced mother) to illustrate "irony" in her English course and discussed the Vietnam War and the draft in one of her freshman-level courses. Students complained that they were unable to understand what Hetrick was trying to teach them, and the head of the English department noted in recommending that Hetrick not be rehired that she discussed unrelated subject matter in class. In ruling on the case, the Court of Appeals asserted,

> *Whatever may be the ultimate scope of the amorphous 'academic freedom' guaranteed to our Nation's teachers and students, it does not encompass the right of a non-tenured teacher to have her teaching style insulated from review by her superiors when they determine whether she has merited tenured status just because her methods and philosophy are considered acceptable somewhere within the teaching profession* (p. 709).

Clark and *Hetrick* indicate that colleges and universities constitutionally can require their faculty to teach subject matter appropriate to the courses that are assigned to them and to adhere to teaching styles and philosophies that are consonant with those of the institution to which they belong.

The 1st Circuit Court of Appeals upheld a university's right to set and maintain academic standards in *Lovelace v. South-eastern Massachusetts University*, 793 F.2d 419 (1st Cir. 1986). The court disagreed that an untenured faculty member's academic freedom and constitutional rights were violated when his contract was not renewed because his grading standards were not in sync with the educational mission of the university. According to the court,

> Whenever a school sets itself up to attract and serve only the best and brightest students or whether instead gears its standards to a broader, more average population is a policy decision which, we think, universities must be allowed to set. And matters such as course content, homework load, and grading policy are core university concerns, integral to implementation of this policy decision (p. 426).

In 1968, the Supreme Court ruled that public employees do not forfeit their First Amendment rights to comment on matters of public interest when they are employed by government.

Clearly, the courts have given colleges and universities the legal authority to establish and maintain the course content and methodologies which they believe are appropriate to their institutional purpose and mission. It is important to note, however, that neither *Clark, Hetrick,* nor *Lovelace* pertained to speech content but rather to questions concerning course content, teaching methods, academic standards, or teaching philosophy. Had these cases pertained to speech content, the legal analysis and constitutional issues involved would have been quite different.

Limitations on freedom in the classroom
Professorial freedom of speech within the classrooms of public higher education institutions has been treated largely as an issue of the rights of public employees to comment on issues of public concern in their capacity as employees of the state. In *Pickering v. Board of Education*, 391 U.S. 563 (1968), the Supreme Court ruled that public employees do not forfeit their First Amendment rights to comment on matters of public interest when they are employed by government.

The difficulty that the court encountered in *Pickering* concerned achieving " . . . a balance between the interests of the (employee), as a citizen, in commenting upon matters of public concern and the interest of the State, as an employer, in promoting the efficiency of the public services it performs through its employees" (p. 568).

To assist in making judgments on this difficult balance, the Supreme Court developed a test in *Pickering.* Essentially, the test analyzed:

1. Whether a close working relationship existed between a state employee and those he or she criticized (in cases where disputes among parties occurred);
2. Whether the subject matter involved was one of legitimate public concern;
3. Whether the speech or communication had a negative impact on the administration of the agency or educational system with which the employee was associated;
4. Whether the employee's daily performance or duties were impeded by his or her comments; and
5. Whether the communication or speech was made as a private citizen or in a professional capacity.

Using this test, the court determined that in the case of Pickering, a public high school teacher dismissed because he criticized the board of education's financial plans in a letter published in the local newspaper, " . . . absent proof of false statements knowingly or recklessly made . . . , a teacher's exercise of his right to speak on issues of public importance may not furnish the basis for his dismissal from public employment" *(Pickering* 1968, p. 574).

While *Pickering* concerned speech outside of the classroom and the balance of a public employee's freedom of speech against the state's interest in maintaining order and efficiency, the case—and specifically the "Pickering test"—was utilized in cases concerning professorial freedom in the classroom. In *Clark v. Holmes,* 474 F.2d 928 (7th Cir. 1972), the untenured faculty member (Clark) claimed that his First Amendment rights were violated in light of *Pickering* after the university refused to rehire him because, among other reasons, he criticized other staff members in his conversations with students.

The federal appellate court denied the applicability of *Pickering* to the case, as Clark's speech did not involve matters of public concern nor were they made in his capacity as a private citizen. The court did, however, utilize the reasoning in *Pickering* to indicate that the university's interest as an employer was greater than the free-speech interest asserted by Clark. In its decision, the appellate court concluded that:

> *The plaintiff here irresponsibly made captious remarks to a captive audience, one, moreover, that was composed of students who were dependent upon him for grades and recommendations. . . . Furthermore,* Pickering *suggests that certain legitimate interests of the state may limit a teacher's right to say what he pleases . . ."* (p. 931).

The 7th Circuit clearly denied that Clark had a free-speech right to criticize those with whom he worked in his interactions with students.

The "Pickering test" was employed but modified in *Connick v. Myers*, 103 S.Ct. 1684 (1983). In *Connick*, the Supreme Court examined whether a constitutional violation of free speech occurred in the discharge of a public employee (Myers), who circulated a questionnaire among employees in her office concerning internal office policies and decisions of which she was critical.

Unlike *Pickering*, the case involved free-speech rights at the workplace and as a public employee. Because the court determined that one of the questions on the questionnaire involved a matter of public concern and was part of the employee's discharge, an examination was necessary to determine whether the discharge was justified constitutionally. Specifically, to determine whether the speech in *Connick* addressed a matter of "public concern," the court had to consider ". . . the content, form, and context of (the speech) . . . as revealed by the whole record" (p. 1,690).

In considering the content of the questionnaire, the court found:

> *. . . is most accurately characterized as an employee grievance concerning internal office policy. The limited First Amendment interest involved here does not require that Connick tolerate action which he reasonably believed would disrupt the office, undermine his authority, and destroy close working relationships. Myers' discharge therefore did not offend the First Amendment* (p. 1,694).

The court noted that the manner, time, and place in which the questionnaire was distributed in the office was relevant. The fact that the questionnaire was created and distributed at the office endangered, in the opinion of the court, the proper functioning of the office.

Further, the court recognized that *Pickering* included ". . . full consideration of the government's interest in the effective and efficient fulfillment of its responsibilities to the public" (quoting paraphrase of *Pickering* in *Connick*, p. 1,692). In considering this part of the "Pickering balance," the Supreme Court noted that "when close working relationships are essential to fulfilling public responsibilities, a wide degree of deference to the employer's judgment is appropriate" (p. 1,692).

Connick underscored the rights of public employers to maintain order and professional relationships in the workplace. While public employees have the right to comment on matters of public concern, they do not have the constitutional right to utilize speech that impedes the proper functioning of the workplace or damages professional working relationships necessary to the proper functioning of their place of employment.

The legal reasoning in *Connick* was employed in a higher education context—and specifically in a case that dealt with a faculty member's classroom speech—in *Martin v. Parrish*, 805 F.2d 583 (5th Cir. 1986). *Martin* involved an untenured economics instructor at Midland College in Texas. The case addressed whether a publicly employed college teacher is protected constitutionally in the abusive use of profanity in the classroom.

The faculty member (Martin) used profane language, including "bullshit," "goddamn," and "sucks," while teaching. Some students complained about the use of such language, and the dean initiated action to terminate Martin's employment. Soon after, the college's board of trustees approved the termination. Martin then brought forward a lawsuit alleging the denial of his First Amendment right of free speech, academic freedom, and right to due process and equal protection.

In analyzing Martin's claims, the 5th Circuit Court of Appeals utilized *Connick* to determine that the content, form, and context of Martin's profanity in the classroom did not address a matter of public concern. In looking at the content, form, and context of his use of profanity, the Court of Appeals found that his speech consisted of comments that criticized the students and the college faculty, but these comments were not used for purposes of instruction relevant to the class.

Moreover, the court determined that Martin's profane speech was not protected because his audience consisted of students who, while in the classroom, were a captive audience unable to easily remove themselves from hearing foul language which had no academic purpose or justification. Using the decision in *Connick*, which supported the rights of public employers to maintain order and discipline in the classroom, the appellate court found that "to the extent that Martin's profanity was considered by the college administration to inhibit his effectiveness as a teacher, it need not be tolerated by the college . . ." (pp. 585-86).

The cases reviewed above indicate that:

- Institutions have significant legal authority over what occurs in the classroom, especially course content, pedagogy, and the right to curtail speech which is unrelated to course content or disruptive of the proper functioning of the institution.
- When faculty speak as public employees and at the worksite, their speech may be curtailed if it does not involve a matter of public concern, destroys close working relationships, disrupts the place of work, or undermines authority.
- To determine whether speech addresses a matter of public concern, the courts must examine the content, form, and context of the speech as revealed by the whole record.

Freedom to Speak as a Citizen

The AAUP's publication, *Policy Documents and Reports* (1990), contains a number of references regarding the rights and obligations of faculty when they speak as citizens. Among the AAUP's central policy documents concerning the freedom to speak as a citizen are the 1940 Statement and the 1970 Interpretive Comments, the Committee A Statement on Extramural Utterances, and the Statement on Professional Ethics. These policy documents are worthy of close attention, as they have been used by federal courts in ruling on cases concerning extramural speech. Moreover, the content of the policy documents once again largely parallels the legal reasoning and decisions of the courts.

The 1940 Statement contains the following language:

College and university teachers are citizens, members of a learned profession, and officers of an educational institution. When they speak or write as citizens, they should be free from institutional censorship or discipline, but their special position in the community imposes special obligations. As scholars and educational officers, they should remember that the public may judge their profession and their institution by their utterances. Hence they should at all times be accurate, should exercise appropriate restraint, should show respect for the opinion of others, and should make every effort to indicate that they are not speaking for the institution (AAUP 1990, p. 4).

The 1970 Interpretive Comments on the 1940 Statement explain further that if the extramural utterances of a faculty member create ". . . grave doubts concerning the teacher's fitness for his or her position . . .," the administration of a college or university can file charges in accordance with specific procedures established within the association's policy section on tenure that deal with faculty dismissal proceedings (AAUP 1990, p. 6).

This position is underscored in the Committee A Statement on Extramural Utterances (approved by Committee A in October 1964) with an additional admonition.

. . . a faculty member's expression of opinion cannot constitute grounds for dismissal unless it clearly demonstrates the faculty member's unfitness to serve. Extramural utterances rarely bear upon the faculty member's unfitness for continuing service . . . In a democratic society freedom of speech is an indispensable right of the citizen. Committee A will vigorously uphold that right (p. 32).

The Statement on Extramural Utterances states also that in cases where a faculty member's speech as a citizen calls into question his or her fitness to serve in the classroom, the final decision on "fitness" should include consideration of the member's complete record in the classroom and as a scholar. Absent "weighty evidence of unfitness," the Statement on Extramural Utterances asserts that the college or university administration should not pursue charges against the faculty member (AAUP 1990, p. 32).

The AAUP Statement on Professional Ethics (endorsed in June 1987) adds that "as citizens engaged in a profession that depends upon freedom for its health and integrity, professors have a particular obligation to promote conditions of free inquiry and to further public understanding of academic freedom" (AAUP 1990, p. 76). This statement and others endorsed by the AAUP on extramural speech emphasize that professors, when speaking as citizens, have the same rights as other citizens. Further, the statements indicate that faculty do have obligations as members of a learned profession to be accurate in what they communicate and to make clear that they are speaking as citizens when they exercise their use of extramural speech. Also, the statements recognize the possibility— however unlikely or difficult to prove—that the extramural speech of a faculty member can show unfitness to serve in the classroom.

Court decisions pertaining to extramural speech largely are consistent with AAUP policy in that they uphold strongly the First Amendment rights of professors to speak as citizens, but recognize that speech outside of the college or university setting can, if exercised with extreme imprudence, create a rare cause for employment termination by the state. In adjudicating extramural-speech cases concerning faculty, the courts use basically the same legal tests and analyses employed in intramural speech cases wherein the free-speech rights of the faculty member are balanced against the rights of the employer in ". . . promoting the efficiency of public services it performs through its employees" (*Pickering v. Board of Education*, 391 U.S. 563 [1968], p. 568).

The primary case utilized in ruling on extramural speech cases is *Pickering* (discussed earlier with regard to classroom speech), which involved a teacher who criticized the school's administration in a published letter. In brief, *Pickering* emphasized that: 1) teachers may not be compelled constitutionally to relinquish their First Amendment rights as a precondition of public employment (theory of unconstitutional preconditions); 2) a balance must be achieved between the ". . . interests of the teacher, as a citizen, in commenting upon matters of public concern and the interest of the state, as an employer, in promoting the efficiency of the public services it performs through its employees" (p. 568); and 3) ". . . a teacher's exercise of his right to speak on issues of public importance may not furnish the basis of his dismissal from public employment" (p. 574).

In balancing Pickering's extramural-speech rights with the interests of the state, the Supreme Court found that Pickering's letter addressed a matter of public concern, and that the letter did not impede his performance in the classroom or disrupt the normal operation of his school. Moreover, in a footnote, the court determined that Pickering's public statements were not so without foundation that his competence as a teacher would be called into question.

The "Pickering balance" was applied in a higher education setting involving extramural speech in *Starsky v. Williams,* 353 F. Supp. 900 (1972). *Starsky* involved an assistant professor at Arizona State University who was discharged by the university board, in part, for speech that he exercised outside of the university campus. In analyzing the content of Starsky's extramural speech, the district court found that Starsky never spoke as a representative of the university nor claimed any expertise that related to his profession.

Further, in employing the Pickering balance, the district court found that the content of Starsky's words ". . . do not include terms of personal abuse as to any specific individuals; that they do not include a call for any immediate, unlawful, or dangerous action, or disruptive conduct" (p. 922). As a result, the court did not find any evidence in Starsky's speech content to indicate that the university's interest outweighed Starsky's free-speech rights. In deciding the case, the court found that:

> . . . the Board, in discharging Professor Starsky on the basis of narrow professional standards of accuracy, respect, and restraint applied to public statements made as a citizen, has violated its own A.A.U.P. standards not to discipline a teacher when he 'speaks or writes as a citizen,' and has violated Professor Starsky's rights to freedom of speech by applying constitutionally impermissible standards to speech made as a citizen . . . the Board confuses constitutionally protected criticism with disrespect (pp. 922, 924).

In summary, faculty enjoy the same extramural speech rights as other citizens as long as:

- They make clear that they are speaking as citizens and not as representatives of their college or university;
- They address matters of public concern; and
- Their speech does not call into question their professional competence or damage the operation or services provided by their college or university.

Summary

Though academic freedom is not explicitly referred to in the language of the Constitution, the Supreme Court recognizes it as a "special concern" of the First Amendment, providing some degree of constitutional protection to faculty at public higher education institutions. Matherne cautions against granting special constitutional stature to academic freedom, since creating such an impenetrable shield would give academic institutions license to do anything (1984).

The Supreme Court often refers to AAUP standards and policies when addressing the legal concerns of academic freedom. The faculty freedoms articulated in the AAUP's 1940 Statement include the freedom to conduct research and publish, teach in the classroom, and speak or communicate as citizens. Surprisingly, institutions have considerable legal control in the classroom over course content and pedagogy and can restrict unrelated or disruptive speech.

Intramural expression regarding legitimate public concern, as opposed to employee concerns, for example, is afforded a greater degree of protection. Faculty enjoy the same freedom to speak extramurally as other citizens, provided their utterances are not so outrageous as to call into question their ability to function as faculty members. The AAUP admonishes faculty to use reasonable judgment during extramural speech and to make clear that the speech is not on behalf of the institution but rather an expression of personal views. The complex area of academic research and publication is fraught with highly charged issues, such as compelled disclosure of data, sponsored research, and protection of confidential sources, that defy legal consensus.

Although the AAUP plays an undeniably critical role in the safeguarding of professorial academic freedoms, their policies rely heavily on the presumption that faculty are self-regulating and can be afforded the highest degree of flexibility. Unfortunately, such lofty aspirations lead sometimes to no-holds-barred policies that fail to take into account scenarios such as excessive profanity in the classroom or publicly displayed photographs depicting child pornography.

For example, the AAUP implies that professors can say anything in the classroom as long as it is within the course subject matter. Does this mean that a faculty member teaching sex education can ask a female student questions about her sexual habits or call attention to her sexual organs? The legal real world is a mix of competing interests: professorial academic freedom, institutional academic freedom, student academic freedom, and society, which at times are in harmony and usually at odds. The next section delves with greater detail into selected controversial topics regarding academic freedom in higher education and offers practical guidance.

CONTEMPORARY ACADEMIC FREEDOM ISSUES

This section examines issues which currently affect academic freedom in the United States including artistic expression, political correctness and hate speech, academic freedom in church-related colleges and universities, and subpoenaed research information. These topics, which vary widely in subject and venue, do not exhaust the academic freedom issues that exist today but do reflect largely the primary intellectual challenges facing higher education institutions in America. Each discussion concludes with recommendations for the evaluation or formulation of policies pertaining to the respective issue.

Artistic Expression

The communication of ideas and concepts is not restricted to the printed word alone but can be achieved also through visual modes such as paintings, drawings, photographs, motion pictures, plays, and sculptures. Artistic expression is exercised throughout college and university campuses—whether in galleries, student centers, classroom or administrative buildings, or outdoors. At times, the expression is innocuous and ignored. At other times, artistic expression arouses passionate response from those who come into contact with it. The display of Robert Mapplethorpe's photographs depicting, in some instances, homosexual themes, generated disparate but generally intense emotions from many who viewed or heard about them.

Artists sometimes intend to provoke emotion and debate by communicating images and ideas which are out of the ordinary, politically sensitive, or perhaps contrary to accepted standards of decency. It is important to note, however, that artistic expression has the capacity to convey ideas and political or social thought just as words on a printed page. Artists, therefore, need academic freedom to convey their message without undue limitations on their intellectual liberty.

Artistic expression can generate questions about the legal and policy parameters in which such expression can be exercised. For example, when is it permissible at a college or university to refuse to display works of art or to suppress an artistic performance? How can higher education administrators exercise judgment in terms of which pieces of art are displayed openly and which others are not to be accorded the same display status? Does artistic expression enjoy constitutional status? What legal considerations are involved, and how

Obscenity is difficult to define because the determination of what is or is not obscene rests largely in the eye of the beholder and in community norms which differ from place to place.

do they affect institutional policy? What rights do faculty members have in displaying their work? Answers to these questions will be addressed by examining the ways in which courts evaluate the legal protection accorded to artistic expression and analyzing the implications of the law for institutional policies and decisions.

Artistic expression and obscenity

Artistic expression sometimes involves questions concerning obscenity. For decades, courts of law have found it exceptionally difficult to define what is or is not obscene. Colleges and universities sometimes face the same problem when works of art that cause discomfort, embarrassment, or anger are displayed, because of the images on canvas, in a photograph, on film, on stage, or through some other medium. Recently, Idaho State University decided to prohibit people who are under the age of 17 from viewing an exhibition of paintings called "Divas and Devils," because the paintings depict partially clothed women (*The Chronicle of Higher Education* March 10, 1993). In other cases, some of which are reviewed here, college and university officials are confronted with provocative works of art that are highly sexual in content and concept.

Obscenity is difficult to define because the determination of what is or is not obscene rests largely in the eye of the beholder and in community norms which differ from place to place. However, Supreme Court decisions offer some measure of assistance in defining obscenity. It is important to note that while artistic expression is protected constitutionally under the First Amendment, the Supreme Court ruled on a number of occasions that obscenity is not protected by the Constitution.

In *Roth v. United States*, 354 U.S. 476 (1957), the Supreme Court made clear for the first time that " . . . obscenity is not within the area of constitutionally protected speech or the press" (p. 485). The definition of obscenity was addressed in *Miller v. California*, 413 U.S. 15 (1973). In *Miller*, Chief Justice Burger set forth guidelines for triers of fact in determining whether something is obscene. Briefly, the guidelines in *Miller* rest on deciding the following:

1. "Whether 'the average person, applying contemporary community standards' would find that the work, taken

as a whole, appeals to the prurient interest."
2. "Whether the work depicts or describes, in a patently offensive way, sexual conduct specifically defined by the applicable state law."
3. "Whether the work, taken as a whole, lacks serious literary, artistic, political, or scientific value" (p. 24).

In *Miller*, the Supreme Court provided some examples of how states may define under the second guideline that which is "patently offensive" sexual conduct. Further, the court underscored the role of each state in providing such a definition, and thereby implicitly acknowledged the multiplicity of standards that would emerge. In *Paris Adult Theatre I v. Slaton*, 413 U.S. 49 (1973), a companion case to *Miller*, the court recognized that states can take a *laissez-faire* approach toward obscenity but constitutionally they can apply stronger standards. Moreover, the standards established by the Supreme Court in *Miller* state (when phrased positively) that a judgment must be made by a trier of fact to see if a work of art contains " . . . serious literary, artistic, political, or scientific value" and, if so, the work may not be dismissed as obscene (O'Neil 1990, p. 179).

Confronting a "trier of fact" is the subjectivity of judgment. While some artistic expression may prove easy to judge obscene, other expression is not so easily labeled. Mapplethorpe's photographs are indicative of the difficulty of deciding whether artistic representations are obscene or protected constitutionally. For example, do nude photographs of adults or children convey a political message or do they contain serious artistic value? Are they obscene? The answers to these questions are difficult and will differ from state to state, community to community, and person to person.

Compounding the difficulty are current changes in the purpose and format of artistic expression which defy the *Miller* analysis. It is noted that:

> . . . Miller *was drafted at a radical turning point in the history of art, and the new art that has arisen since* Miller *has rendered standards such as 'serious artistic value' obsolete. This new art—postmodern art—rebels against the demand that a work of art be serious, or that it have any traditional 'value' at all.* Miller*, then, evaluates contemporary art by*

the very standard which that art seeks to defy (Adler 1990, p. 1,359).

Changing artistic standards may require, therefore, changing standards in legal analyses of what constitutes obscenity or "serious artistic value."

The courts have not provided any appreciable clarification or elaboration of obscenity standards as contained in *Miller*. The *Miller* definition of obscenity continues to be the one that " . . . reigns supreme to this day" (Adler 1990, p. 1,361). While *Pope v. Illinois*, 481 U.S. 497 (1987), added a new dimension to the third guideline in *Miller* by stating that the "proper inquiry is . . . whether a reasonable person would find (serious) value in the material," the basic elements of *Miller* remain intact. Public colleges and universities should continue then to use *Miller* as the guiding case in evaluating whether works of art are obscene as defined by the Supreme Court.

Artistic expression and constitutionally protected speech

Although the Supreme Court decided that obscenity is not protected constitutionally, the court and lower federal courts recognize that some artistic expression is protected by the Constitution. While " . . . the Supreme Court has never defined precisely the scope of First Amendment protection for the creative and performing arts" (O'Neil 1990, p. 178), court decisions do exist which shed light on protected artistic expression including that which occurs in public colleges and universities.

A variety of court cases suggest that " . . . art that conveys a political message or theme stands markedly higher in the constitutional order than art that is 'merely art,' however great its critical acclaim or its aesthetic appeal" (O'Neil 1990, p. 181). Two cases involving public higher education institutions demonstrate the rights of individuals to view artistic expression and the protections afforded artists against the suppression of ideas that are found offensive on political or religious grounds. In *Brown v. Board of Regents of University of Nebraska*, 640 F. Supp. 674 (D. Neb. 1986), authorities at a theater owned and operated by the University of Nebraska-Lincoln cancelled the showing of a scheduled movie titled "Hail Mary" after a state senator expressed opposition to the film. The senator noted that the film (which she had not seen but had heard and read about) was blasphemous of the birth of Christ and the portrayal of Mary (thereby offending the senator's religious beliefs and those of some of her constituents) and could cause demonstrations by those who found the film objectionable.

In deciding the case in favor of those who protested the cancellation of the film, the district court noted that "university students were denied the right to receive the controversial ideas expressed in the film 'Hail Mary' because its content was officially characterized as offensive" (p. 681). Accordingly, the court found that expression was unconstitutionally denied and stated that "Hail Mary" must be reinstated in the theater's schedule. The legal principles underlying *Brown*—that ideas (including those expressed artistically) may not be repressed in a public institution simply because they are found offensive to the political or religious sensitivities of some—are found also in *DiBona v. Matthews*, 269 Cal. Rptr 882 (Cal.App. 4th Dist. 1990).

In *DiBona*, a community college teacher and a former student asserted in part that their free-speech rights were violated when college administrators cancelled a drama class where a controversial play was selected for performance. In finding for the plaintiffs, the court noted that the cancellation of the drama class by college administrators was caused by 1) opposition to the play by members of the religious community, 2) sensitivity of the play's subject matter given a local criminal trial that involved a comparable subject matter, and 3) the belief that the play's language was "inappropriate" (p. 889). Further, the court found that college officials grew interested in the content of the drama class—and specifically the play "Split Second"—only after community opposition was expressed. According to the court:

> As to the 'politically sensitive' nature of the play's subject matter, not only is it a constitutionally inappropriate reason for censorship, ultimately it may also be counterproductive for the community. A central premise of the constitutional guarantee of free speech is that difficult and sensitive political issues generally benefit from constructive dialogue of the sort which may have been generated by "Split Second" (p. 891).

The defense of the courts in protecting artistic expression which conveys a political message or social theme does not equate automatically to a defense of all artists whose work may contain some communicative elements. Involved in court decisions are considerations of the venue in which artistic expression is practiced. The performance of a play may take place in a location where attendance is by consent only—those who attend voluntarily enter a theater to view the performance and can leave easily if they so desire. However, some artistic expression, such as the display of paintings or photographs, may be located in an area where viewing is involuntary—such as in buildings with a high degree of pedestrian traffic. These cases raise issues worthy of closer examination, as they pertain to legal questions that colleges and universities address with some regularity.

Display art

What rights do faculty members or others have in displaying their work in colleges and universities? Under what conditions may the display of faculty art be denied or restricted in public institutions of higher learning? These are not hypothetical questions but ones that higher education leaders confront with increased frequency. Two cases help in responding to these questions: *Close v. Lederle*, 424 F.2d 988 (1970), and *Piarowski v. Illinois Community College*, 759 F.2d 625 (1985).

In *Close*, the 1st Circuit Court of Appeals considered whether the removal of a University of Massachusetts art instructor's paintings from the corridor of the university's student union violated his First and 14th Amendment rights. In examining and weighing the rights of the instructor and the university officials, the court looked first at whether the instructor's art sought to express political or social thought.

The court noted that several of the paintings in the instructor's exhibit were " . . . nudes, male or female, displaying the genitalia in what was described as 'clinical detail.' A skeleton was fleshed out only in this particular. One painting bore the title, 'I'm only 12 and already my mother's lover wants me.' Another, 'I'm the only virgin in my school'" (p. 990). The court found, therefore, that "there is no suggestion, unless in its cheap titles, that plaintiff's art was seeking to express political or social thought" (p. 990). The instructor's constitutional interests in displaying his paintings in the university student union were thereby found "minimal" (p. 990).

Next, the court looked at the university officials' interest to see if it justified the removal of the paintings. Here, the court noted that the corridor where the sexually explicit paintings were displayed was used on a regular basis by the public, including children. The court found the university officials justified in considering the ". . . primary use to which the corridor was put" and in determining that the paintings were inappropriate to that use (p. 990). Given that the corridor was used heavily by the public, the court asserted that "where there was, in effect, a captive audience, defendants had a right to afford protection against 'assault upon individual privacy'" (p. 990).

The balance, then, between the instructor's interest in exhibiting his art and the university's interest in preventing the involuntary viewing of sexually explicit paintings in a heavily traveled part of the campus swung in favor of the university. In this regard, the court noted that "freedom of speech must recognize, at least within limits, freedom not to listen" (p. 991).

Comparable facts but a different institutional solution are presented in *Piarowski v. Illinois Community College*, 759 F.2d 625 (1985). In *Piarowski*, the chairman of the art department at Prairie State College claimed that various college officials violated his First Amendment rights by ordering him to relocate certain pieces of his art to a different site on the campus. The 7th Circuit Court of Appeals analyzed the location where the art was displayed, the content of the art, questions concerning the professional position of the artist at the college, and what did or did not constitute a public forum.

As in *Close*, the court in *Piarowski* found that the college's "gallery" where the art was displayed adjoined the "mall" on the main floor of the principal building on campus. Nothing separated the gallery from the mall, and the mall served as the college's primary thoroughfare and gathering place. It was in this setting that the art in question was displayed and caused complaints from students, staff, and others.

The court then examined the content of the art. The art contributed by the chairman of the art department (Piarowski) consisted of eight stained-glass windows. Three of the windows generated controversy and complaints. According to the court:

One depicts the naked rump of a brown woman, and stick-

ing out from (or into) it a white cylinder that resembles a finger but on closer examination is seen to be a jet of gas. Another window shows a brown woman from the back, standing, naked except for stockings, and apparently masturbating. In the third window another brown woman, also naked except for stockings and also seen from the rear, is crouching in a posture of veneration before a robed white male whose most prominent feature is a grotesquely out-sized phallus . . . that the woman is embracing (p. 627).

The court noted that "Piarowski intended no political statement by the content and coloring used in his windows, no disparagement of women or blacks, no commentary on relations between the sexes or between the races. The windows were art for art's sake" (p. 628).

After they were displayed in the gallery for 10 days, college officials ordered Piarowski to remove the windows and recommended that he exhibit them in a fourth-floor room of the building where the art department classrooms were located. After Piarowski refused to move the windows, a college official removed them.

In finding for the college officials, the court was moved by several considerations. First, the artistic expression was not political in nature. Second, the artistic expression was "regulated rather than suppressed" (p. 632). Moreover, the college argued persuasively that the art would make difficult efforts to recruit students and demonstrated that the art was visible to people who never entered the gallery (O'Neil 1990), thus making them, as in *Close*, the unwilling recipients of offensive material.

These cases are instructive in that they caused consideration of whether it is the "medium" or the "setting" of art displayed in galleries which are constitutionally determinant (O'Neil 1990, p. 185). "Despite the uncertain status given the creative arts in both cases, the critical factor seems to be the *location* of the exhibit . . . " (O'Neil 1990, pp. 185, 186). Colleges and universities are able to change the venue of a work of art that may prove offensive to the public and place it in a location where it may still be seen—but only by willing observers. In *Close* and *Piarowski*, the courts respected the decision of college officials in removing sexually explicit works of art from highly used areas on campus. However, had these two cases involved art that conveyed political messages, the legal analysis would have been more difficult, as political expression is protected above "art for art's sake."

Artistic expression and the AAUP

The AAUP's Committee A on Academic Freedom and its council endorsed in June 1990 a statement on academic freedom and artistic expression. The statement offers not only a defense of artistic expression but also a series of "proposed policies" for institutions. The policies are intended to provide some assistance to colleges and universities in upholding academic freedom within the visual and performing arts and in responding to issues which might emerge as a result of the public display or presentation of artistic expression (AAUP 1990).

The AAUP Statement of Academic Freedom and Artistic Expression contains four proposed policies which can be summarized as follows:

1. Academic Freedom in Artistic Expression: Those involved in the visual and performing arts are entitled to and need academic freedom as much as those who produce other forms of academic work or expression. As artistic expression is an integral part of the academic environment, it is important that "educational and artistic criteria should be used by all who participate in the selection and presentation of artistic works" (AAUP 1990, p. 35). The AAUP asserts also that "reasonable content-neutral regulation of the 'time, place, and manner' of (artistic) presentations should be developed and maintained. Academic institutions are obliged to ensure that regulations and procedures do not impair freedom of expression or discourage creativity by subjecting artistic work to tests of propriety or ideology" (p. 35).

2. Accountability: Institutions that display artistic work or provide venues for performances do not necessarily endorse the artistic presentations. Moreover, the artists do not necessarily represent the institution wherein their works are displayed or performed. Artists should not present their work or themselves as "speaking for the Institution" (p. 36).

3. The Audience: Institutions that display art or serve as the location for performances should protect the rights of the artists and those who attend from those who may be

opposed to the exhibit or performance.
4. Public Funding: Art and colleges and universities that are funded by public revenue heightens the responsibility of institutions of higher learning to uphold academic freedom and of the public to " . . . respect the integrity of academic institutions. Government imposition on artistic expression of a test of propriety, ideology, or religion is an act of censorship which impermissibly denies the academic freedom to explore, teach, and to learn" (p. 36).

The AAUP statement contains some policy guidance for institutions in providing environments that uphold academic freedom for artistic expression, but the statement largely ignores the difficulties that sometimes arise concerning such expression. For example, the statement's "proposed policies" do not recognize the difficult issue of obscenity and institutional rights legally to prohibit the display of such material or the placement of sexually explicit depictions in areas that are beyond the view of those who do not wish to see them.

The language of the statement is vague where it indicates that institutions may "reasonably" indicate which places are available for artistic display or performance. It is not clear what "reasonably" means to the AAUP, but institutions are well-advised to seek policy guidance from the court cases that have analyzed the legal rights of institutions and artists concerning artistic expression. The AAUP contends that it is an " . . . act of censorship . . . " for the government to place on artistic freedom any " . . . test of propriety, ideology, or religion . . . " but does not recognize that some artistic expression will create extreme difficulty for colleges and universities to display or allow performed.

For example, is it within the acceptable limits of AAUP policy for an institution to deny the performance of "Old Calcutta" in its auditorium or to prohibit the display of photographs of men and women engaged in sexual activity? Total artistic freedom is not possible in colleges and universities. While the Supreme Court and the lower courts recognize that artistic expression, particularly that which conveys a political message, does have some constitutional protection, there are legally permissible limitations on artistic freedom and the display of works of art.

Policy recommendations and considerations
To the extent possible, colleges and universities should protect freedom of expression and the exchange of ideas. Artistic
expression will, at times, present institutional challenges when
such expression offends a large portion of the academic community and the public. There are, however, ways to preserve
the communication of ideas artistically to the fullest extent
possible and in a manner that is open and fair to artists and
those who observe their work. Moreover, guidance is provided through court decisions which can assist institutions
in the formulation of policy pertaining to artistic expression.

   The following considerations and recommendations may
prove useful to institutions in formulating policy:

1. Artistic expression which conveys political or social
    thought is given a higher level of constitutional protection
    than "art for art's sake."
2. Artistic expression that is obscene is not protected
    constitutionally.
3. The location in which art is displayed on campus may be
    regulated in such a way that people may not involuntarily
    see some art (such as that which is sexually explicit).
4. Institutions should develop clear artistic and educational
    guidelines regarding the selection of artistic works that
    are displayed on campus. The guidelines should be easily
    accessible to members of the college or university.
5. Colleges and universities may post a statement at the
    entrance of a gallery or theater or in a display or perfor-
    mance program indicating that the artistic expression is
    not necessarily endorsed by the institution nor does the
    artist represent the views of the institution.
6. Colleges and universities may indicate through a posted
    notice that the artistic expression contained in a gallery
    or performance is sexually explicit and potentially inap-
    propriate for viewing by children.
7. Institutions can designate an alternate site for the display
    of sexually explicit—but not obscene—material.
8. Colleges and universities may preserve freedom of expres-
    sion and thought by coinciding the display or performance
    of highly provocative artistic expression with campus-wide
    seminars, debates, or other forms of discussion on the
    subject or topic presented through the artistic expression.

Political Correctness

Political correctness, like obscenity, is difficult to define. How one defines and interprets it depends largely on personal perspective and experience. Gender, race, political orientation, and other complex factors enter into the role of "political correctness" in the United States and in the country's colleges and universities. This segment examines briefly the different ways in which political correctness is defined or perceived, how it is manifested in the American academic community, and how it relates to academic freedom.

Political correctness is now a part of the American lexicon as demonstrated by its inclusion in the *Random House Webster's College Dictionary* (D'Souza 1991a). There, it is defined as being "marked by or adhering to a typically progressive orthodoxy on issues involving especially race, gender, sexual affinity or ecology" (D'Souza 1991a, p. xiv). Another source notes that "generally speaking, it is used to describe a belief system that discourages the expression or harboring of certain ideas" (Conciatore 1991, p. 8).

The term "political correctness" defies easy definition because the definitions are highly charged by political and social orientation. For some, it is defined and perceived in repressive tones that emphasize conformity and restrictions on expression. For others, it represents a positive force that heightens sensitivity toward individuals or groups that historically were or are made to conform to the views and values of an insensitive majority. Common in the definitions or perceptions is the concept of repression. However, there is no concensus as to the source of repression within the multitude of definitions.

For example, one observer notes, "what I think it (political correctness) has come to mean for a large part of the public is a way of perceiving, particularly in academic life, that requires conformity to a certain set of views and that is willing to punish non-conformity" (In Conciatore 1991, p. 8). Another observer states, " . . . I perceive 'political correctness' as closer, often, to 'political corruption,' for what is obvious is that power corrupts even where there has been an exchange of power in the name of justice" (Lewis 1991, p. 5). These views perceive repression as spreading outward from a group that seeks to change by force the expressed views and values of those who hold (or historically have held) a majority view. In other words, repression is emanating outward from groups within larger society.

A different view, however, perceives repression as moving from larger society inward toward smaller groups that may have different views and values. As one writer notes:

Some of the extraordinary tensions evident on campuses these days stem from attempts to impose universalist ideas of community that stress consensus and shared values on a situation in which differences seem fundamental and irreducible. The universalist idea assumes that some common denominator of interest allows 'us' to articulate our common concerns and regulate our disagreements; those who do not accept the consensus are necessarily outside the community (Scott 1991, p. 30).

In physical terms, these different views of political correctness can be categorized as being either explosive or implosive.

In physical terms, these different views of political correctness can be categorized as being either explosive or implosive. The explosive view perceives conformity as moving outward from a subset of society onto all of society, whereas in the implosive view conformity folds inward from a powerful majority of society onto those who have different values and ideas.

Some view political correctness as destructive of respectful give and take inside and outside the classroom. Reports are made of students complaining of "pressure to subscribe to 'politically correct' opinions corresponding to the ideological orthodoxies of groups claiming to have been victimized" (D'Souza 1991, p. B1). Reports abound also of teachers being chastised or dismissed because of seemingly innocent comments made in the classroom and of pressure to reorient the content of the curriculum to accommodate minority views (D'Souza 1992). Still others voice the opposing side by claiming that what is taught and how it is taught reflects the repression of differing views and perspectives. One observer of political correctness and the curriculum notes that:

A crucial point, one regularly overlooked in hysterical pronouncements about the takeover of the curriculum, is that power is unequally distributed: those demanding change must contend with disciplinary and pedagogic practices that are institutionalized, command resources, and claim to have truth, rigor, and objectivity on their side (Scott 1991, p. 37).

The AAUP does not view the "political correctness" issue as being a fundamental threat to academic freedom. The association views criticism of political correctness as emanating from " . . . an only partly concealed animosity toward equal opportunity and its first effects of modestly increasing the participation of women and racial and cultural minorities on campus" (AAUP September/October 1991, p. 48). The association's "Statement on the 'Political Correctness' Controversy" states firmly that there is no "contradiction" between academic freedom and the AAUP policy on affirmative action and equal opportunity. While one would hardly expect a contradiction between the association's conception of academic freedom and its own statement on affirmative action and equal opportunity, the AAUP fails to recognize that some manifestations of political correctness can jeopardize academic freedom. Moreover, the association disclaims any parallel between the repressive atmosphere of McCarthyism and the discomfort on campuses that is raised by political correctness.

Absent from the AAUP's "Statement on the 'Political Correctness' Controversy" is the open acknowledgment and understanding of the difficulties that political correctness can create for those in intellectual communities. If colleges and universities are places for the free exchange of ideas and opinions then ideas and opinions, which are distasteful to the political or social norms of the institutions must be allowed in the "marketplace of ideas."

In its most basic form, the very term "political correctness" implies the existence of something politically incorrect—that which if espoused or endorsed may cause harm by those who wield influence or power. The resulting fear of being penalized by expressing a certain view or idea leads naturally to the impulse of withholding ideas from the marketplace. Those who risk the expression of politically incorrect views may find that it exacts a high price—including loss of position or employment. This creates a dilemma for the academic community. The dilemma is how to create an environment where ideas and points of view are welcome as part of the give and take of the intellectual enterprise and, simultaneously, to recognize that some views will be unpopular and perhaps offensive.

Two recent examples demonstrate the difficulties that colleges and universities face when faculty express radical or unpopular opinions. Both examples involve faculty at City

College of the City University of New York who made highly provocative statements outside of the classroom. In one case, a tenured professor of philosophy, Michael Levin, made public statements and wrote about his belief that black people are inferior intellectually to whites. Levin also expressed controversial views regarding feminism and homosexuality. When Levin later sued City College, claiming that he was punished for his extramural statements on black people, the district court ruled in his favor.

In the second case, a tenured professor of black studies, Leonard Jeffries Jr., was removed from his position as chairman of the black studies department at City College after he made a controversial off-campus speech that many deemed racist in content. In his speech, Jeffries asserted that Jews and the Mafia worked together to portray blacks in a negative way in movies. Jeffries also called a professor of mathematics at City College the "head Jew" and expressed his belief that wealthy Jews financed the slave trade (Magner 1993, p. A18).

Jeffries sued officials at City College following his removal from the chairmanship of black studies department. A federal jury found in Jeffries' favor despite claims made by the college that Jeffries' comments would prove harmful to the black studies department. The jury found no evidence to that effect, and the district court judge ruled that Jeffries' free-speech rights were, in this particular case, of greater importance than the college's rights and interests in maintaining efficient operations (Magner 1993).

As in these two cases, personal points of view sometimes will be found offensive. However, the exchange of ideas must remain as open as possible on colleges and universities so that learning and intellectual discovery are not impeded unnecessarily. On rare occasion, a faculty member's expression may prove so bizarre or hateful as to call into question professional competency. In such cases, as indicated above, due-process procedures can be implemented to evaluate whether or not the faculty member can function adequately as a teacher.

The political correctness issue appears largely to revolve around issues of respect and the recognition of diversity in human experience, history, and values. Recognition of diversity entails the parallel recognition that individuals sometimes will express ideas or points of view that are distasteful or offensive to others. Colleges and universities sometimes are

placed in the difficult position of protecting distasteful speech so that ideas which are unpopular are not censored from places where thought and knowledge are valued and examined.

In the classroom, a faculty member's verbal communication of subject matter and interactions with students conveys a variety of messages. Professional norms of conduct as stated by the AAUP in its "Statement on Professional Ethics" emphasize that professors are to " . . . demonstrate respect for students as individuals" and to encourage the "free pursuit of learning" among students (AAUP 1990, p. 76). Moreover, the professor is to " . . . exercise critical self-discipline and judgment in using, extending, and transmitting knowledge" (pp. 75, 76). College and university faculty are to respect individual students, encourage their pursuit of knowledge, and convey knowledge in a professional manner. In terms of the content of classroom subject matter, faculty are admonished in the AAUP's 1940 Statement to be "careful not to introduce into their teaching controversial matter which has no relation to their subject" (AAUP 1990, p. 3). In sum, what is to be taught is material or knowledge pertinent to the subject, and how it is to be taught is in a manner that respects individual students.

Students also have responsibilities in the classroom. In a "Joint Statement on Rights and Freedoms of Students" endorsed by the AAUP in 1967, it is stated that "students should be free to take reasoned exception to the data or views offered in any course of study and to reserve judgment about matters of opinion, but they are responsible for learning the content of any course of study for which they are enrolled" (AAUP 1990, p. 154). Disagreement is permitted in the classroom, but it is to be "reasoned," and matters of personal opinion that are expressed within the classroom are to be respected.

Some speech, such as that which incites violence, need not be protected by colleges and universities. "Hate speech" is emerging as a well-recognized term in the academy and beyond. The term refers to speech that " . . . has come to embrace the use of speech attacks based on race, ethnicity, religion, and sexual orientation or preference" (Smolla 1990, p. 195). For example, hate speech may arise during a gay or lesbian march on campus if those with different sexual orientations launch abusive verbal attacks on those marching. In such cases, a reasoned debate is not occurring on the issue of differences in sexuality, but rather verbal attacks are being levied on people who have different sexual preferences.

There are, in such cases, legal and policy issues that can come into play of which college and university faculty and administrators should be aware. "The only prohibitions (on hate speech) likely to be upheld are narrowly drawn restrictions on fighting words that present a clear and present danger of violence, or that punish physical injury to persons or property, or illegal discriminatory conduct, or that involve purely private speech in a context completely removed from discussion of general or public concern" (Smolla 1990, p. 216). Speech in public colleges and universities is protected constitutionally and may not be silenced or punished in a higher education faculty context because it offends others.

Hate speech, if practiced in the classroom, could, in extreme forms and cases, present institutional leaders with reason to discipline or dismiss such faculty. If, for example, a professor espousing neo-nazi values stated that Jews as a race should be eliminated from the earth, such statements could be used as proof that the faculty member was unfit to serve in the classroom. In such a case, relationships with other faculty and students could be harmed irreparably and limit the capacity of the professor to perform teaching and advising functions adequately. "The members of the faculty act as the representatives of the university in the classroom both on matters intellectual and on matters not plausibly related to intellectual positions. The university is under a constitutional obligation to refrain from stigmatizing hate speech and may likewise require the faculty, as its representatives, to refrain from stigmatizing hate speech in the classroom" (Smolla 1990, p. 222).

Colleges and universities can take protective measures to emphasize a respect for diversity while protecting academic freedom. The following measures are recommended:

1. State clearly in faculty manuals and student publications that student and faculty diversity and the diversity of opinions are valued elements of academic and campus life;
2. Define clearly in faculty and student publications the components of faculty and student academic freedom and make clear that diversity of opinion and academic freedom are harmonious concepts worthy of vigilant protection;

3. Reinforce in faculty and student orientation sessions that respect for diversity and opposing viewpoints is an essential element in the exchange of ideas and the pursuit of knowledge;
4. State clearly in faculty and student publications that while the freedom to express ideas and beliefs will be respected, conduct and behavior that result in the defacement of property, physical intimidation of others, or the disruption of campus activities will be subject to penalty (See AAUP 1992 "On Freedom of Expression and Campus Speech Codes," p. 31); and
5. Make known that due-process procedures will be followed in all cases where charges of faculty or student misconduct are levied.

Academic Freedom in Church-Related Colleges and Universities

The issue of academic freedom in church-related colleges and universities continues to be debated in higher education in the United States. Members of the higher education community who experience or observe the conflict over the relationship between religious doctrine and academic freedom—and their respective purposes—express the need to question intellectually the role, purpose, and existence of academic freedom in their particular church or denomination (Curran 1986; Godsey 1987).

The ambiguity and confusion that envelop academic freedom in some church-related colleges and universities results from incomplete policy statements and the failure to place academic freedom within the context of religious systems of thought. The policy documents and reports of the AAUP do not address how academic freedom can survive in church-related institutions without imperiling ecclesiastic missions or goals or compromising the integrity of the academic profession.

AAUP policies and church-related colleges and universities

This segment analyzes the AAUP's policy statements on academic freedom on church-related colleges and universities; the disjuncture between the AAUP conception of academic freedom and the tenets of religious institutions; and the importance and examples of policy clarity in independent colleges.

The AAUP's "Statement on Academic Freedom in Church-Related Colleges and Universities" (1967) appears to remain just a "draft statement" and is not included in the association's 1990 *Policy Documents and Reports.* Moreover, the 1940 Statement on academic freedom does not address sectarian interests beyond what is commonly referred to as the limitations clause, stating that "limitations of academic freedom because of religious or other aims of the institution should be clearly stated in writing at the time of the appointment" (AAUP 1990, p. 3). The AAUP's 1970 Interpretive Comments of the 1940 Statement state in reference of the limitations clause that "most church-related institutions no longer need or desire the departure from the principle of academic freedom implied in the 1940 Statement, and we do not now endorse such a departure" (AAUP 1990, p. 6).

The 1970 Interpretive Comment on church-related institutions is highly presumptuous and overly simplistic. It implies that the AAUP knows definitively whether church-related colleges and universities need a departure from academic freedom as defined by the association and refuses to consider the possibility that different constructions of "truth" and "ways of knowing" exist in academe. A church-related college or university may hold sacred certain values or beliefs and, through faith, consider such values and beliefs—such as the existence and teachings of Jesus Christ—truth itself. Also, faith or divine revelation and not necessarily research alone may be considered the "way of knowing" certain information. This perhaps is illustrated most easily in the field of theology. If one is studying the theology of the Lutheran Church as a faculty member and ordained minister at a seminary, certain core beliefs such as the belief in the Trinity will be considered truth through faith or divine revelation and not open to question. The AAUP 1970 Interpretive Comments do not recognize that such core values and beliefs may cause some institutions either to limit the freedoms contained in the 1940 Statement or to create or adopt a different conception of academic freedom.

The 1970 Interpretive Comments imply also that the AAUP definition of academic freedom should override institutional academic freedom in deciding which values and beliefs the college, university, or seminary elects to uphold through its affiliation with a church. The reason for different denominations and the multitude of church-related colleges and universities that are spread throughout the United States is the desire to be identified with certain values and beliefs. Presbyterians are Presbyterians and not Lutherans for a reason—they have some values and beliefs that are different from other groups or organizations.

Academic freedom, as defined by the AAUP, could, if adopted without modification, remove the distinct identity of a church-related institution as it welcomes calling into question the fundamental tenets of the church. A faculty member at a Southern Baptist institution who questioned or opposed adult baptism would, in effect, be questioning or attacking the values and identity of the Southern Baptist Convention that contributed funds for the institution's support and operation.

The college, university, or seminary's interest may, in such cases, be to preserve its religious identity by not adopting the AAUP 1970 Interpretive Comments. "To impose the secular norm of academic freedom on unwilling religious colleges and universities would increase the homogeneity—and decrease the vitality—of American intellectual life" (McConnell 1990, p. 304). Institutional academic freedom—the freedom to chart an institutional course and identity without external interference—does not seem valued by the AAUP within its verbiage on church-related institutions of higher learning.

Whereas the AAUP tends to emphasize the academic freedom of individuals, the courts—and particularly the Supreme Court—tend to recognize institutional academic freedom (McConnell 1990). One of the most stark examples of the Supreme Court's recognition of institutional academic freedom appeared in *Sweezy v. New Hampshire*, 354 U.S. 234, 263 (1957) where Justice Frankfurter wrote that academic freedom entailed ". . . the four essential freedoms of a university—to determine for itself on academic grounds who may teach, what may be taught, how it shall be taught, and who may be admitted to study" (See also McConnell 1990, pp. 305, 306). Frankfurter's conception of academic freedom is a better fit for church-related institutions than the AAUP 1940 Statement and 1970 Interpretive Comments, as it recognizes the *institution's* right to establish and maintain a distinctive academic identity. The maintenance of a distinctive academic identity depends in large measure on clarity in institutional policies and contracts.

Policies and contracts in church-related colleges and universities

As mentioned in the previous section, the legal differences between private and public colleges and universities must be kept in mind when examining academic freedom in church-related colleges and universities. As private entities, church-related colleges and universities and their faculties are not under the purview of constitutional law. Rather, faculty in such institutions must rely mainly upon the provisions in their contracts for the legal protection and definition of academic freedom.

> We tend to assimilate the (academic freedom) claims of persons in public and private institutions although lawyers are quite clear that the Bill of Rights reaches the private sector only in what is 'state action.' For the most part, faculty and others in private campuses must depend upon non-constitutional safeguards (O'Neil 1984, p. 250).

As the legal relationship between church-related colleges and universities is heavily dependent upon contracts, it is important that academic freedom policies and teaching contracts be understood clearly by faculty and administrators. Where policy ambiguity exists, faculty cannot know with certainty what rights or freedoms they have to conduct research, publish, teach, or speak extramurally. This, in turn, can lead to either faculty hesitation to pursue and share scholarship for fear of offending institutional or church leaders or to faculty using policy ambiguity as an excuse for deviating from intended institutional limits on academic freedom. Policy clarity can, on the other hand, serve to provide faculty with clearly delineated parameters on academic freedom—thus removing confusion and uncertainty—and institutions with the means of retaining their church-related identity.

Faculty handbooks, teaching contracts, and denominational policies pertaining to academic freedom in church-related colleges and universities vary widely in their policy clarity and content (Poch 1990). Some are specific in the expectation that denominational beliefs or doctrine will be upheld and honored in the academic life and work of an institution. For example, the Lutheran Church–Missouri Synod (LCMS) endorses a statement titled "Limitation on Academic Freedom" which is applicable to LCMS-related higher education

Where policy ambiguity exists, faculty cannot know with certainty what rights or freedoms they have to conduct research, publish, teach, or speak extramurally.

institutions.

Faculty members are pledged to the Scriptures as the inspired and inerrant Word of God and to the Lutheran Confessions. They are expected to honor, to uphold, and to teach in accordance with the synodically adopted doctrinal statements which express the convictions of the fathers and brethren with whom all members of the Synod are united in the obedience to the Scriptures and the Confessions (Concordia Seminary—"Faculty Employment Agreement [untenured faculty], Exhibit A, "Policy Statement on Limitation of Academic Freedom").

The requirements contained in this statement are made part of faculty contracts in LCMS higher education institutions. To elaborate further on the meaning of this limitation statement, Concordia Seminary includes as an "exhibit" in its faculty employment agreement a statement of clarification to assure teachers that:

to honor, to uphold, and to teach in accordance with the synodically adopted doctrinal statements does not require faculty members to avoid discussion, examination, and elucidation of opinions at variance with the Synod's doctrinal position. Indeed, it is the board's wish that opinions and doctrinal positions contrary to the synodically adopted doctrinal statements be fairly presented, discussed, and evaluated on the basis of the Scriptures and the Lutheran Confessions (Concordia Seminary *Faculty Handbook*, p. 4.027).

This statement is not resistant to the presentation of ideas contrary to those held doctrinally by the LCMS nor is the language of the "Limitation on Academic Freedom" statement. Faculty in LCMS institutions are, however, pledged through mandatory membership in the church to uphold Lutheran doctrine and the confessional statements in their teaching, research, and publishing. The "Limitation on Academic Freedom" statement and the "exhibit" in the employment contract quoted here provide faculty with an understanding of the limitations that are, as a result of their employment at an LCMS institution, placed upon their academic freedom. This understanding is enhanced further by the LCMS *Handbook*, which lists as part of a contractual relationship with faculty "all the Symbolical

Books of the Evangelical Lutheran Church (which) as a true and unadulterated statement and exposition of the Word of God" are expected to be honored and adhered to in teaching, research, and publication (LCMS 1986, p. 9).

Common among some church-related institutions is the endorsement of the AAUP 1940 Statement either by name or by endorsing the content of the statement without reference to the AAUP (Poch 1990). Church-related institutions which do not limit academic freedom as defined by the 1940 Statement generally are those which are ecumenical in orientation, thus valuing commonalities among all believers rather than the defense of specific church dogma. For example, colleges and universities related to the Lutheran Church in America (LCA), Presbyterian Church (U.S.A.), and the United Methodist Church frequently have no limitations on academic freedom as defined by the AAUP, as those three denominations are ecumenical in orientation. When the orientation of the sponsoring church is ecumenical, the desire for unity rather than the survival of individual sects results in less restrictive academic freedom policies and increased academic flexibility.

One LCA-related institution states in its faculty handbook that while "the teacher should be committed to the objectives of Christian liberal-arts education . . . this does not require subscription to narrowly sectarian views or unquestioning assent to dogma" (Poch 1990, p. 203). This policy statement implies that faculty have some flexibility in the presentation or expression of ideas and concepts, as faculty are not restricted academically by any church dogma. However, the statement also does not indicate clearly what faculty freedoms exist or whether the institution does or does not endorse the AAUP definition of academic freedom verbatim or in modified form.

Institutions which restrict academic freedom because of strongly held beliefs often state their academic freedom policies more specifically than do those who do not restrict such freedom because of their ecumenical orientation or an absence of church dogma. Whether restrictive or permissive, academic freedom policies should be specific so that faculty can know contractually the parameters within which they can teach, research, publish, and speak extramurally. The absence of clearly stated policies can result in academic freedom disputes and legal entanglements such as those which emerged between Father Charles E. Curran and The Catholic University of America.

Academic freedom and the case of Charles Curran at The Catholic University of America

The dramatic and unusual academic freedom case of Father Charles E. Curran, dismissed professor of moral theology at The Catholic University of America (CUA), was followed closely by the American press and largely misinterpreted by journalists and the public. The severe misinterpretation of the case—caused mainly by ignorance of the unique history and structure of CUA and Charles Curran's place within it— makes worthy some brief discussion of the case here.

Most often, descriptions of Curran's civil lawsuit with CUA focused on national legal-oriented issues. However, a major and critically significant aspect of Curran's multifaceted case virtually went unnoticed. One of the most important elements of Curran's case was not national but international in scope. The unique structure of CUA and Curran's position within that structure—both symbolic and tangible—gave his academic freedom case an important international dimension. Before discussing this, it is important to understand Curran's views as a Catholic theologian and how such views led to his dismissal as a professor of moral theology.

Curran's belief that non-infallible teachings of the church hierarchy are open to debate, reinterpretation, and public dissent placed him in direct confrontation with the Vatican and led to his removal from the theological faculty of CUA. He emphasizes the fundamental need for theologians to question authoritative, but non-canonical, statements of the church by asserting that "the theological reason for dissent rests on the epistemological recognition that on specific moral questions one cannot leave that degree of certitude which excludes the possibility of error" (Curran 1982, p. 370). To rephrase it, Curran is convinced that certain issues such as homosexuality or abortion are so complex that they elude definitive and comprehensive single answers. Curran believes that epistemological questions entail the constant possibility of error and, therefore, the possibility of legitimate dissent.

Curran's interpretation of what specific moral questions are open to theological exploration, interpretation, and debate are those which Vatican officials claimed were close enough to the "core" of the faith to warrant full acceptance and integration within the global Catholic community. Those theological issues on which Curran and the Vatican collided most violently included homosexuality, contraception, abortion, masturbation, and divorce. Curran wrote treatises and delivered speeches openly which attempted to fathom exegetically the theological boundaries of such topics. In the process, he developed a body of interpretive literature deemed inappropriate and in serious doctrinal error by the Congregation for the Doctrine of the Faith.

Curran's 20-year persistence in proclaiming the right to dissent from non-infallible teaching proved costly. Though defended by acclaimed theologians, national theological societies, and Catholic higher education organizations, Curran no longer is permitted to teach theology in the name of the Roman Catholic Church in Vatican-accredited degree programs.

In 1986, the Congregation for the Doctrine of the Faith determined that Curran no longer was "suitable or eligible to exercise the function of a professor of Catholic theology." This decision came after a nine-year investigation of Curran's articles and books by the Congregation and active correspondence between the two parties.

At no other Catholic college or university in the United States would Curran have needed a papal mandate or license to teach theology. However, if Curran were to teach theology at any one of the hundreds of Vatican-accredited programs located virtually throughout the world, he would need such a mandate, as do his international colleagues.

One cannot separate Curran's case from the anomalous qualities of The Catholic University within American higher education. Unlike any other Catholic college or university within the United States, CUA was chartered under the direct guidance and approval of the pope. Since its establishment in April 1887 under Pope Leo XIII, the university continues to retain its link to the Vatican—albeit in different form.

At its inception, all university academic programs contained within the School of Sacred Sciences came within the purview of the Vatican. The university's academic programs now are organized within nine schools and one college. Seven of the nine schools are governed entirely by "civil bylaws which are now the effective governing document of the university" and do not have "canonical status"—i.e., the power to grant degrees in disciplines founded upon church law. Direct papal control remains only upon the "Faculties" of the School of Philosophy and the departments of Canon Law and Theology, both of which are within the School of Religious Studies

("Canonical Statutes of the Ecclesiastical Faculties of The Catholic University of America," p. 1).

The distinction between Catholic institutions that are under the purview of ecclesiastical authorities and those that are not—largely an international versus national distinction—was highlighted in February 1986 within the response of the Association of Catholic Colleges and Universities' board of directors (elected by officials in American Catholic colleges and universities) to a "Proposed SCHEMA for a Pontifical Document on Catholic Universities." A small portion of the response is quoted here to demonstrate further the link between the Curran case and Catholic colleges and universities that exist internationally as contrasted with the governance structure of those that exist within the United States.

> In the section (of the SCHEMA) which delineates the various ways in which universities may be 'Catholic,' there is no category which describes our institutions. In each case there seems to be the assumption of a juridical tie with either the Holy See or the local Ordinary. Most of our colleges and universities have no such link; they were established by communities of religious men or women who secured charters from the several states empowering them to confer degrees. They have seen, and still see, their Catholic character and mission as residing in their commitment to establish and assure a Christian presence in the university world (Association of Catholic Colleges and Universities 1986, p. 2).

Therefore, a vital aspect of Curran's case—the loss of his license to teach theology within Vatican-accredited programs—has relatively little meaning or significance within the United States, as it bars him only from teaching that discipline in one Catholic university and less than a dozen seminaries out of approximately 235 Catholic colleges and seminaries that exist nationally.

The ramifications of the Curran case are more formidable internationally. While no one appears certain of the precise number of Catholic institutions with Vatican-licensed faculties—including the Vatican's own Sacred Congregation for Catholic Education—the general number appears large. There are approximately 17 pontifical universities and faculties within Rome alone. In general terms, these institutions are united by the common purpose of training men for the priesthood and exploring the parameters of Roman Catholic doctrine. Most fundamentally, however, they are linked by their common relationship to the Vatican through papal teaching licenses and the attendant purview of the Sacred Congregation for the Doctrine of the Faith.

Vatican action in the Curran case is not an insular occurrence, for decisions made as to the role of the theologian and the purpose and limits of dissent transcend national borders as does the Roman Catholic Church itself. The fact that a Roman Catholic theologian in the United States was removed from a canonically erected faculty by an order issued from the Vatican City in Rome is an effective demonstration of Vatican authority extending across political and cultural boundaries.

Conclusions and Recommendations for Church-Related Institutions

As national professional education-related organizations generally are not equipped to provide specific policy guidance on matters relating to professorial freedom within religious systems of thought, it is important that church-related colleges and universities state clearly what freedoms are or are not available to the faculty. Specifically:

1. Limitations on academic freedom because of the relationship of a college, university, or seminary to a church should be stated clearly within contractual documents. Academic freedom policy should be explained fully in a faculty handbook or formal teaching contract—whether limited or not—so that institutional members understand the degree of freedom available to them in the four component areas specified by the AAUP (i.e., the freedom to teach, research, publish, and speak extramurally). Policy ambiguity may lead to faculty inhibition because of the fear of trespassing intellectually on forbidden areas of inquiry. If colleges, universities, or seminaries endorse the AAUP's 1940 Statement, the Association of Theological Schools' statement on academic freedom and tenure, or other policies, they should be quoted in contractual documents and not simply referenced.
2. Church-related institutions that endorse the AAUP's 1940 Statement should indicate whether the "limitation clause" (i.e., "limitations of academic freedom because of reli-

gious or other aims of the institution should be clearly stated in writing at the time of the appointment") is or is not operative with faculty contractual documents. Colleges, universities, and seminaries that quote the AAUP's 1940 Statement in its entirety but do not elaborate upon or address the limitation clause leave faculty uncertain about the proper interpretation of the statement. Institutions should either state that no limitations are in place because of religious affiliation or place a clearly framed statement of limitation contiguous to the 1940 Statement.

3. Teaching contracts that are signed by faculty upon acceptance of a position should include, at minimum, reference to applicable academic freedom policies in relevant policy documents of the college, university, or seminary. If no academic freedom policy exists within a church-related institution, that fact also should be explicit in the contract.

Subpoenaed Information and Protected Sources

Rik Scarce, a published sociologist and a graduate student at Washington State University, is in jail. Scarce was jailed for refusing to comply with a district court subpoena. The subpoena ordered him to testify before a federal grand jury about the vandalism of university laboratories by animal rights activists (Monaghan 1993b). While Scarce did not participate in the vandalism, his research on animal rights activists and particularly his friendship with one of the suspects in the destruction of a Washington State University laboratory led to his subpoena. His refusal to indicate whether he had conversations with a primary suspect in the vandalism case placed him in contempt of court and, as a result, in jail. Rik Scarce's case provides reason to consider the issue of subpoenaed research information and some pragmatic questions of which scholars should be mindful when conducting research.

As a researcher, Scarce is not alone in facing difficulties caused by compelled testimony. For decades, scholars supplied information and materials under court order. A 1976 survey showed that over the period of one decade, some 50 subpoenas were given to university faculty demanding that they provide research materials (O'Neil 1983). The effects on academic freedom are dramatic. Compelled testimony or disclosure of research information (including results) carry the potential of damaging publication opportunities and chilling access to research material (O'Neil 1983. See also

Labaton 1987).

As one East Asian scholar remarked two decades ago:

> *My observation is that a subpoena has an effect of intim-*
> *idation both on the person subpoenaed and on those who*
> *might have contact with him. I can testify from personal*
> *knowledge that in the early 1950s . . . the widespread sub-*
> *poena of China scholars had the public effect of inhibiting*
> *realistic thinking about China, and I believe the result car-*
> *ried over into unrealistic thinking about Chinese relations*
> *with Vietnam and helped to produce our difficulties there*
> (O'Neil 1983, p. 851, quoting John K. Fairbank).

Given the potentially dramatic affect of subpoenaed information on academic freedom, what can researchers do to provide the most effective protection of their research material?
In short, what practical advice can be provided to scholars
and institutions concerning compelled testimony and the
need to protect confidential sources? These questions are
addressed below.

As stated in the previous section, balancing the rights of
researchers and the protection of their scholarship and
sources with judicial needs for information to adjudicate cases
produces a tension that sometimes is difficult to resolve.
Moreover, this balance must be addressed with each case, as
the issues and circumstances differ (Monaghan 1993A). Some
practical considerations, however, can be valuable to academic
researchers who may encounter subpoenas for research information. While legal precedent via a review of some of the central cases involving subpoenas of academic research was discussed in the previous section, this segment is intended to
provide practical guidance—and a list of elements to consider—to researchers who may well be challenged with subpoenas. A brief discussion of each follows.

1. The probative value of research material. One central consideration that can emerge in cases involving subpoenaed
   research information is the importance of the research
   to the case at hand (O'Neil 1983). At times, a researcher
   who is not a party to a lawsuit can demonstrate that other
   sources of comparable information exist that can be utilized for purposes of adjudicating a case and, in the process, prevent the disclosure of personal research records

or data (See, for example, *Richards of Rockford, Inc. v. Pacific Gas & Elec. Co.*, 71 F.R.D. 388 [N.D. Cal. 1976]. See also O'Neil 1983, p. 844).

2. The burden of compliance. When researchers or institutions are subpoenaed to provide information, they can seek some relief for such requests as providing information within very short time spans and complying with court orders which entail significant expense or large quantities of information. For example, a researcher at Mount Sinai Medical School in New York City was subpoenaed to provide more than 18,500 medical records which filled 97 file drawers in 19 cabinets and 250 bound volumes. The medical school challenged the subpoena and prevailed, as the court found compliance with the subpoena too oppressive on the researcher and school (Holder 1986).

Further, measures to control the scope of compliance can be sought, so that the burden or harm of providing research information can be minimized. In *United States v. John Doe*, 460 F.2d 328, 332 (1st Cir. 1972), a case involving the distribution of the Pentagon Papers, a scholar claimed that disclosure of certain information would harm irreparably his capacity to function as a researcher. In light of this claim, the Court of Appeals for the 1st Circuit responded in a way that ". . . although the scholars were ordered to testify, they were not required to provide confidential information acquired in the course of a researcher-subject relationship" (Holder 1986, p. 407. See also O'Neil 1983, p. 849). Moreover, some research information that is highly confidential in nature—such as biomedical research—can be modified under the direction of a court so that identifiers are removed to protect research subjects (See, for example, *Deichtman v. Squibb & Sons*, 740 F.2d 556 [7th Cir. 1984]).

3. Research in progress. A scholar whose materials are subpoenaed while his or her work is in progress has a stronger claim to not disclose the materials as they may not have been tested or validated, and premature disclosure can prove harmful to publication and other professional opportunities. In *Dow Chem. Co. v. Allen*, 672 F.2d 1262 (7th Cir. 1982), the Court of Appeals for the 7th Circuit recognized the potential for professional damage that could emerge from the premature disclosure of research information.

*If a private corporation can subpoena the entire work prod-
uct of months of study, what is to say, further down the line,
the company will not seek other subpoenas to determine
how the research is coming along? To these factors must be
added the knowledge of the researchers that even inadver-
tent disclosure of the subpoenaed data could jeopardize
both the studies and their careers. Clearly, enforcement of
the subpoenas carries the potential for chilling the exercise
of First Amendment rights* (Quoted in O'Neil 1983, pp. 850,
851).

It should be understood, however, that research in progress
is not a sure defense against a subpoena, as demonstrated
by the case of *Deichtman v. Squibb & Sons,* 740 F.2d 556 (7th
Cir. 1984).

4. Research subject matter. The subject of research may influence significantly the degree of legal protection that the
   research material receives when under the force of subpoena. For example, research on rhesus monkeys or on
   automobiles likely will have a lower degree of protection
   than will research pertaining to human subjects. Subpoenaed information on cancer patients or human sexuality
   will involve matters of personal confidentiality not found
   in research on animals or inanimate subjects. Some argue
   that ". . . the confidentiality of human subjects of biomedical research should be held inviolate" (Holder 1986,
   p. 406). While such a statement may prove unworkable
   legally, it is certain that the confidentiality of biomedical
   research material is protected more effectively than research material where confidentiality is not promised or
   pertinent.

5. Promise of and reasons for confidential sources. Some
   forms of research, including some biomedical research
   involving humans, create situations where there is an obligation of the researcher to the subject to maintain confidentiality concerning the identity of the research subject.
   This fiduciary relationship generally is respected in medical research as patients' medical records are personal and
   confidential. "In most states, a treating physician may not
   be forced to testify against or about a patient without the
   patient's permission" (Holder 1986, p. 412).

To claim a confidential source, researchers must meet the
criteria that they told the subjects that they would keep the
source of information secret, that secrecy was essential to the

relationship, that the relationship between the source and researcher was important to the community, and that the injury of disclosure outweighs the benefits of disclosure (O'Neil 1983). While confidentiality is not always guaranteed, courts often make provisions to protect the identity of sources of research information. In *Diechtman v. Squibb & Sons,* 740 F.2d 556 (7th Cir. 1984), records were made available but without personal identifiers.

    6. Civil versus criminal cases. Whether a case involves a civil or criminal lawsuit can affect the effectiveness of a researcher to resist compelled disclosure of research information and material. A researcher is more likely to be forced to comply with a subpoena in a criminal case. In a criminal case, a researcher may possess information that is critical to the defense of a suspect or, as in the case of Rik Scarce at Washington State University, may have information that could lead to a criminal conviction.

The previous discussion suggests that researchers and institutions consider the following:

1. When human subjects are involved in a study, researchers and subjects should anticipate that the research information may be subpoenaed. Researchers can have human subjects agree to allow the researchers to make information available provided that no personal identifiers are included. Moreover, researchers can gather research information in such a way as to expedite providing the information without the names of human subjects. For example, a cover sheet on research information may have a patient's name, but subsequent sheets may have only identifier numbers rather than name and are invaluable in biomedical research where litigation occurs with some frequency. Such strategies can save researchers enormous amounts of time, as documents with names will not have to be modified if subpoenaed.
2. Institutions should anticipate that researchers may be subpoenaed and develop guidelines so that the institutions and researchers can respond effectively. For example, researchers should be cautious about volunteering to serve as "expert witnesses," as such volunteerism can cause the researchers' notes to become opened for purposes of cross-examination and possibly cause the institution some legal liability (Holder 1986).

CONCLUSIONS AND RECOMMENDATIONS

Academic freedom is essential to unfettered intellectual inquiry in colleges and universities. Faculty freedom to teach, research, publish, and speak extramurally are necessary to advance knowledge without fear of institutional retribution. Moreover, clearly articulated statements on academic freedom and the visible support of college and university leaders are critical to the perpetuation of academic freedom in institutions of higher learning.

For college and university faculty, academic freedom as defined by the AAUP enables free discourse to take place within the classroom and outside of the institution and new realms of knowledge to be explored and disseminated through scholarly research and publication. Quality scholarship and teaching often depend largely on institutional environments where free inquiry is valued and supported by trustees, college and university presidents, and the faculty themselves. Restrictions on academic freedom which are not articulated clearly at the time of faculty appointment can lead to teaching and scholarship marked by timidity and, therefore, the stagnation of learning and inquiry.

The value and importance of academic freedom for faculty are echoed largely for institutions as a whole. Clearly worded academic freedom principles and policies dedicated to the advancement of scholarship and learning provide a reasoned position from which to act when intellectual liberty is jeopardized or threatened by external forces. For example, church-related institutions need coherent and comprehensible academic freedom policies when ecclesiastical authorities external to the colleges or universities attempt to restrict faculty speech or scholarship. The absence of academic freedom policies leaves institutions of higher learning and their faculty vulnerable to a variety of external threats.

The following recommendations are intended to provide some guidance in the protection of faculty academic freedom:

1. Public and independent colleges and universities should include in faculty handbooks an official policy statement on academic freedom that specifies what freedoms are available to faculty members. If the institution endorses the AAUP 1940 Statement, the statement should be printed in full in the faculty handbook. Moreover, if the statement is endorsed, the institution should indicate whether the 1970 Interpretive Comments are endorsed also. Any re-

Quality scholarship and teaching often depend largely on institutional environments where free inquiry is valued and supported by trustees, college and university presidents, and the faculty themselves.

strictions on academic freedom should be stated clearly and completely in the faculty handbook and provided as part of the teaching contract.

2. Church-related colleges and universities should make a special effort to specify for faculty members what the relationship is between their institutions and the churches that help to support them. Denominational colleges and universities may have regulations based upon church affiliation that can restrict academic freedom. For example, the Lutheran Church–Missouri Synod has as a provision in its *Handbook* that a faculty member may be removed for "advocacy of false doctrine or failure to honor and uphold the doctrinal position of the Synod . . ." (The Lutheran Church–Missouri Synod 1986, p. 109). Such provisions should be made known to faculty members at the time of their appointment.

3. Senior-level administrators in public colleges and universities should be familiar with the constitutional parameters of faculty academic freedom so that the legal rights and responsibilities of all members of the college or university community may be preserved. The dynamics of competing freedoms will challenge campus leaders to make the difficult decisions that should be based upon a knowledge of the legal aspects of intellectual freedom.

4. Faculty should be involved actively in the development of institutional policies that affect academic freedom. Such policies may involve statements on such topics as artistic expression and political correctness. Faculty participation can assist in minimizing unforeseen harm to academic freedom, as faculty are involved directly with the conveyance of knowledge to students and are engaged in research, publishing academic work, and, at times, in speaking to groups external to the institutions. Their experience in the broad spectrum of intellectual activity can prove invaluable to policy makers as they develop and act upon academic freedom policies.

Clear faculty policies and a respect for the diversity of opinions and values of the members of a college or university community will go far toward protecting and perpetuating academic freedom. The freedom to teach, research, publish, and speak extramurally enhances the exchange of ideas and contributes to an effective learning environment.

REFERENCES

The Educational Resources Information Center (ERIC) Clearinghouse on Higher Education abstracts and indexes the current literature on higher education for inclusion in ERIC's data base and announcement in ERIC's monthly bibliographic journal, *Resources in Education* (RIE). Most of these publications are available through the ERIC Document Reproduction Service (EDRS). For publications cited in this bibliography that are available from EDRS, ordering number and price code are included. Readers who wish to order a publication should write to the ERIC Document Reproduction Service, 7420 Fullerton Rd., Suite 110, Springfield, VA 22153-2852. (Phone orders with VISA or MasterCard are taken at 800-443-ERIC or 703-440-1400.) When ordering, please specify the document (ED) number. Documents are available as noted in microfiche (MF) and paper copy (PC). If you have the price code ready when you call EDRS, an exact price can be quoted. The last page of the latest issue of *Resources in Education* also has the current cost, listed by code.

"Academic Freedom and the Law." 1936-37. *The Yale Law Journal* 46: 670-86.

Adler, Amy. 1990. "Post-Modern Art and the Death of Obscenity Law." *The Yale Law Journal* 99: 1,359-78.

American Association of University Professors. November-December 1983. "Statement of the Wingspread Conference on Evaluation of Tenured Faculty." *Academe* 69: 14a.

———. 1984. *Policy Documents and Reports.* Washington, D.C.: American Association of University Professors.

———. July-August 1990. "Academic Freedom and Artistic Expression." *Academe* 76: 13.

———. July-August 1991. "Mandated Assessment of Educational Outcomes." *Academe* 77: 49-56.

———. September-October 1991. "Statement on the 'Political Correctness' Controversy." *Academe* 77 (5): 48.

Boudin, Leonard B. 1983. "Academic Freedom: Shall We Look to the Court?" In *Regulating the Intellectuals,* edited by Craig Kaplan and Ellen Schrecker. New York: Praeger.

Brubacher, John S., and Willis Rudy. 1976. *Higher Education in Transition: A History of American Colleges and Universities, 1636-1976.* 3d rev. ed. New York: Harper and Row.

Cecil, Joe Shelby, and Robert Boruch. 1988. "Compelled Disclosure of Research Data." *Law and Human Behavior* 12(2): 181-89.

Conciatore, Jacqueline. May 23, 1991. "Political Correctness: A New Tyranny or a Dangerous Diversion?" *Black Issues in Higher Education* 8: 1+.

Curran, Charles E. 1982.

———. 1986. *Faithful Dissent.* Kansas City, Mo.: Sheed & Ward.

D'Souza, Dinesh. April 24, 1991. "In the Name of Academic Freedom, Colleges Should Back Professors Against Students' Demands for

'Correct' Views." *Chronicle of Higher Education* 38(32): B1+.

―――. 1992. *Illiberal Education: The Politics of Race and Sex on Campus.* Vintage Books edition. New York: Vintage Books.

Eby, Frederick, and Charles Flinn Arrowood. 1940. *The History and Philosophy of Education Ancient and Medieval.* Englewood Cliffs, N.J.: Prentice-Hall, Inc.

Eisenberg, Rebessa S. 1988. "Academic Freedom and Academic Values in Sponsored Research." *Texas Law Review* 66: 1,363-1,404.

Garraty, John A., and Peter Gay, eds. 1972. *The Columbia History of the World.* New York: Harper and Row Publishers.

Godsey, R. Kirby. October 16, 1987. "The Meaning of a Baptist University." *The Mercer Cluster.* 9.

Hackney, Sheldon. July-August 1990. "The NEA Under Attack: Resisting the Big Chill. *Academe* 76(4): 14-17.

Handbook of the Lutheran Church–Missouri Synod. 1986. St. Louis: The Lutheran Church–Missouri Synod.

Haskins, Charles Homer. 1957. *The Rise of Universities.* Ithaca and London: Cornell University Press.

Herberg, Will, et al. 1971. *On Academic Freedom,* edited by Valerie Earle. Washington, D.C.: American Enterprise Institute.

Hofstadter, Richard, and Walter P. Metzger. 1955. *The Development of Academic Freedom in the United States.* New York: Columbia University Press.

Hofstadter, Richard, and Wilson Smith. 1961. *American Higher Education: A Documentary History.* 2 vols. Chicago: The University of Chicago Press.

Holder, Angela R. 1986. "The Biomedical Researcher and Subpoenas: Judicial Protection of Confidential Medical Data." *American Journal of Law and Medicine* XII (3 & 4): 405-22.

"Idaho State U. Accused of Censoring Local Artists." March 10, 1993. *Chronicle of Higher Education:* A5

Kaplin, William A. 1985. *The Law of Higher Education.* San Francisco: Jossey-Bass.

Katz, Kathryn D. Summer 1983. "The First Amendment's Protection of Expressive Activity in the Classroom: A Constitutional Myth." *U.C. Davis Law Review* 16(4): 857-932.

Lewis, Florence C. Fall 1991. "A Report from the PC Front." *The College Board Review* 16(4): 2-7.

Licata, Christine M. 1986. *Post-tenure Faculty Evaluation: Threat or Opportunity?* ASHE-ERIC Higher Education Report No. 1. Washington, D.C.: Association for the Study of Higher Education. ED 270 009. 118 pp. MF-01; PC-05.

Matherne, J. Graham. 1984. "Forced Disclosure of Academic Research." *Vanderbilt Law Review* 37: 585-620.

May, William W., ed. 1987. *Vatican Authority and American Catholic Dissent.* New York: Crossroad.

―――. July-August 1988. "Academic Freedom in Church-related

Universities." *Academe.*

McConnell, Michael W. Summer 1990. "Academic Freedom in Religious Colleges and Universities." *Law and Contemporary Problems* 53(3): 303-24.

Monaghan, Peter. April 7, 1993. "Facing Jail, a Sociologist Raises Questions About a Scholar's Right to Protect Sources." *Chronicle of Higher Education*: A10.

———. May 26, 1993. "Sociologist Is Jailed for Refusing to Testify About Research Subject." *Chronicle of Higher Education*: A10.

Murphy, William P. 1964. "Academic Freedom—An Emerging Constitutional Right." In *Academic Freedom*, edited by Hans W. Baade. Dobbs Ferry, N.Y.: Oceana Publications, Inc.

Olswang, Steven G., and Barbara A. Lee. 1984. *Faculty Freedoms and Institutional Accountability: Interactions and Conflicts.* ASHE-ERIC Higher Education Report No. 5. Washington, D.C.: Association for the Study of Higher Education. ED 252 170. 90 pp. MF-01; PC-04.

O'Neil, Robert M. 1983. "Scientific Research and the First Amendment: An Academic Privilege." *U.C. Davis Law Review* 16(94): 837-55.

———. 1984. "Academic Freedom and the Constitution." *Journal of College and University Law* 3: 275-92.

———. 1990. "Artistic Freedom and Academic Freedom." *Law and Contemporary Problems* 53(3): 177-94.

Pincoffs, Edmund L., ed. 1972. *The Concept of Academic Freedom.* Austin: University of Texas Press.

Poch, Robert K. 1990. "Academic Freedom Policies in Selected Christian Colleges, Universities, and Seminaries." Ph.D. dissertation, University of Virginia.

Pritchett, C. Herman. 1971. "Academic Freedom and the Supreme Court: Is Academic Freedom a Constitutional Right?" In *Academic Freedom*, edited by Valerie Earle. Washington, D.C.: American Enterprise Institute for Public Policy Research.

Rudolph, Frederick. 1962. *The American College and University: A History.* New York: Vintage Books.

Schrecker, Ellen. 1986. *No Ivory Tower: McCarthyism and the Universities.* New York and Oxford: Oxford University Press.

Scott, Joan Wallach. November-December 1991. "The Campaign Against Political Correctness: What's Really at Stake?" *Change* 23(6): 30-43.

Smolla, Rodney A. Spring 1990. "Academic Freedom, Hate Speech, and the Idea of a University." *Law and Contemporary Problems* 53(3): 195-226.

Strohm, Paul. July-August 1990. Academic Freedom and Artistic Expression." *Academe* 76(4): 7-12.

Tewksbury, D.G. 1932. *The Founding of American Colleges Before the Civil War.* New York.

Van Alstyne, William. 1972. "The Specific Theory of Academic Freedom and the General Issue of Civil Liberty." In *The Concept of Academic Freedom*, edited by Edmund L. Pincoffs. Austin: University of Texas Press.

———. 1984. *Interpretations of the First Amendment.* Durham, N.C.: Duke University Press.

———. 1990. "Academic Freedom and the First Amendment in the Supreme Court of the United States: An Unhurried Historical Review." *Law and Contemporary Problems* 53(3): 79-154.

Veysey, Laurence R. 1965. *The Emergence of the American University.* Chicago: The University of Chicago Press.

Wesson, Marianne, and Sandra Johnson. May-June 1991. "Post-Tenure Review and Faculty Revitalization." *Academe* 77(3): 53-57.

Wiebe, Robert H. 1967. *The Search for Order, 1877-1920.* New York: Hill and Wang.

Yudof, Mark G. Winter 1987. "Three Faces of Academic Freedom." *Loyola Law Review* 32(4): 831-51.

Court Cases

Branzburg v. Hayes, 408 U.S. 665 (1972).

Brown v. Board of Regents of University of Nebraska, 640 F. Supp. 674 (D. Neb. 1986).

Clark v. Holmes, 474 F.2d 928 (1972).

Close v. Lederle, 424 F.2d 988 (1970).

Connick v. Myers, 461 U.S. 138 (1983).

Cooper v. Ross, 472 F. Supp. 802 (1979).

DiBona v. Matthews, 269 Cal. Rptr 882 (Cal. App. 4th Dist. 1990).

Deitchman v. Squibb & Sons, 740 F.2d 556 (7th Cir. 1984).

Dow Chemical Co. v. Allen, 672 F.2d 1262 (7th Cir. 1982).

Everson v. Board of Education, 350 U.S. 1 (1947).

Farnsworth v. Proctor & Gamble, 104 F.R.D. 335 (N.D. Ga. 1984).

Gray v. Board of Higher Education, 92 F.R.D. 87, 90 (S.D. N.Y. 1981); rev'd, 692 F.2d 901 (2d. Cir. 1982).

Greene v. Howard University, 412 F.2d 1128 (1969).

Hetrick v. Martin, 480 F.2d 705 (1973).

In re: *Dinnan*, 661 F.2d 426 (5th Cir. 1981).

James v. Board of Education of Central Dist. No. 1, Etc., 46 F.2d 566 (1972).

Keyishian v. Board of Regents, 385 U.S. 589 (1967).

Lovelace v. Southeastern Massachusetts University, 793 F.2d 419 (1st Cir. 1986).

Martin v. Parrish, 805 F.2d 583 (1986).

Miller v. California, 413 U.S. 15 (1973).

Mt. Healthy City Board of Ed. v. Doyle, 429 U.S. 274 (1977).

Parducci v. Rutland, 316 F. Supp. 352 (1970).

Piarowski v. Illinois Community College, 759 F.2d 625 (1985).

Pickering v. Board of Education, 391 U.S. 563 (1968).

Rampey v. Allen, 501 F.2d 1090 (1974).

Regents of the University of Michigan v. Ewing, 747 U.S. 214 (1985).
Richards of Rockford, Inc. v. Pacific Gas and Electric Co., 71 F.R.D.
    388 (N.D. Cal. 1976).
Roth v. United States, 354 U.S. 476 (1957).
Shelton v. Tucker, 364 U.S. 479 (1960).
Slochower v. Board of Education, 350 U.S. 551 (1956).
Smith v. Lossee, 485 F.2d 334 (1973).
Starsky v. Williams 512 F.2d 109 (1975).
Sweezy v. New Hampshire, 354 U.S. 234 (1957).
The Trustees of Dartmouth College v. Woodward, 17 U.S. 518 (1819).
United States v. John Doe, 460 F.2d 328 (1st Cir. 1972).
United States v. O'Brien, 391 U.S. 367 (1969).
University of California Regents v. Bakke, 438 U.S. 265 (1978).
Wieman v. Updegraff, 344 U.S. 183 (1952).
Wright v. Jeep Corp., 547 F. Supp. 871 (E.D. Mich. 1982).

INDEX

A

AAC. See Association of American Colleges

AAUP. See American Association of University Professors

AAUP Policy Documents and Reports

B

C

I
Idaho State University, 42
Interflex program, 21

J
Jeffries, Leonard Jr., 55

K
Kaplin, William, xv
Keyishian, 19
Keyishian v. Board of Regents, xv. 18-19, 24

L
Law of Higher Education, xv
LCA. See Lutheran Church of America
LCMS. See Lutheran Church-Missouri Synod
Lehrfreiheit, 6-8
Lernfreiheit, 6
Levin, Michael, 55
Limitation on Academic Freedom, 61-63
Lovelace v. Southeastern Massachusetts University, 30, 31
Lutheran Church
        Missouri Synod, 61-62, 74
        of America, 63
        related institutions, 6, 59
        see also Evangelical Lutheran Church

M
Mapplethorpe, Robert, 41, 43
Martin v. Parrish, 34-35
Methodist-related institutions, 5-6
Midland College, 34
Miller v. California, 42-44
Mount Sinai Medical School, 70

N
National Board of Medical Examiners, 21
NBME. See National Board of Medical Examiners
New York Education Law, 19
New York (state), 19
Northern Illinois University, 30

O
obscenity definition and guidelines, 42-43
Old Calcutta performance, 50
old-time college era, 6
Oxford, 4

Stevens, Justice, 21
student freedom
        AAUP Rights and Freedoms of Students (1967), 56
        absence of discussion (1915), 9
subpoena
        of information criteria, 26-27
        practical guidance for researchers, 69-72
Sweezy, Paul, 17-18
Sweezy v. New Hampshire, 17, 19, 24, 29, 60

U
United Methodist Church, 63
United States
        Court of Appeals, 21, 30-31, 33-34, 47, 70
        Supreme Court, 16, 20-23, 31-32, 42-44, 50, 60
        v. John Doe, 70
universitas in Middle Ages, 3
University of California
        at Davis, 20
        Regents v. Bakke, 20
University of
        Chicago, 8
        Massachusetts, 46
        Michigan, 21
        Nebraska-Lincoln, 44
        New Hampshire, 17-18
        New York, 19
        Wisconsin, 8

V
Vietnam War, 30

W
Warren, Chief Justice, 17-18
Washington State University, 68, 72
Wright v. Jeep Corp., 27

ASHE-ERIC HIGHER EDUCATION REPORTS

Since 1983, the Association for the Study of Higher Education (ASHE) and the Educational Resources Information Center (ERIC) Clearinghouse on Higher Education, a sponsored project of the School of Education and Human Development at The George Washington University, have cosponsored the *ASHE-ERIC Higher Education Report* series. The 1993 series is the twenty-second overall and the fifth to be published by the School of Education and Human Development at the George Washington University.

Each monograph is the definitive analysis of a tough higher education problem, based on thorough research of pertinent literature and institutional experiences. Topics are identified by a national survey. Noted practitioners and scholars are then commissioned to write the reports, with experts providing critical reviews of each manuscript before publication.

Eight monographs (10 before 1985) in the ASHE-ERIC Higher Education Report series are published each year and are available on individual and subscription bases. Subscription to eight issues is $98.00 annually; $78 to members of AAHE, AIR, or AERA; and $68 to ASHE members. All foreign subscribers must include an additional $10 per series year for postage.

To order, use the order form on the last page of this book. Regular prices are as follows:

Series	Price	Series	Price
1993	$18.00	1985 to 87	$10.00
1990 to 92	$17.00	1983 and 84	$7.50
1988 and 89	$15.00	before 1983	$6.50

Discounts on non-subscription orders:
- Bookstores, and current members of AERA, AIR, AAHE and ASHE, receive a 25% discount.
- Bulk: For non-bookstore, non-member orders of 10 or more books, deduct 10%.

Shipping costs are as follows:
- U.S. address: 5% of invoice subtotal for orders over $50.00; $2.50 for each order with an invoice subtotal of $50.00 or less.
- Foreign: $2.50 per book.

All orders under $45.00 must be prepaid. Make check payable to ASHE-ERIC. For Visa or MasterCard, include card number, expiration date and signature.

Address order to
ASHE-ERIC Higher Education Reports
The George Washington University
1 Dupont Circle, Suite 630
Washington, DC 20036
Or phone (202) 296-2597
Write or call for a complete catalog.

1993 ASHE-ERIC Higher Education Reports

1. The Department Chair: New Roles, Responsibilities and Challenges
   Alan T. Seagren, John W. Creswell, and Daniel W. Wheeler

2. Sexual Harassment in Higher Education: From Conflict to Community
   Robert O. Riggs, Patricia H. Murrell, and JoAnn C. Cutting

3. Chicanos in Higher Education: Issues and Dilemmas for the 21st Century
   by Adalberto Aguirre, Jr., and Ruben O. Martinez

1992 ASHE-ERIC Higher Education Reports

1. The Leadership Compass: Values and Ethics in Higher Education
   John R. Wilcox and Susan L. Ebbs

2. Preparing for a Global Community: Achieving an International Perspective in Higher Education
   Sarah M. Pickert

3. Quality: Transforming Postsecondary Education
   Ellen Earle Chaffee and Lawrence A. Sherr

4. Faculty Job Satisfaction: Women and Minorities in Peril
   Martha Wingard Tack and Carol Logan Patitu

5. Reconciling Rights and Responsibilities of Colleges and Students: Offensive Speech, Assembly, Drug Testing, and Safety
   Annette Gibbs

6. Creating Distinctiveness: Lessons from Uncommon Colleges and Universities
   Barbara K. Townsend, L. Jackson Newell, and Michael D. Wiese

7. Instituting Enduring Innovations: Achieving Continuity of Change in Higher Education
   Barbara K. Curry

8. Crossing Pedagogical Oceans: International Teaching Assistants in U.S. Undergraduate Education
   Rosslyn M. Smith, Patricia Byrd, Gayle L. Nelson, Ralph Pat Barrett, and Janet C. Constantinides

1991 ASHE-ERIC Higher Education Reports

1. Active Learning: Creating Excitement in the Classroom
   Charles C. Bonwell and James A. Eison

2. Realizing Gender Equality in Higher Education: The Need to Integrate Work/Family Issues
   Nancy Hensel

3. Academic Advising for Student Success: A System of Shared Responsibility
   Susan H. Frost

4. Cooperative Learning: Increasing College Faculty Instructional Productivity
   David W. Johnson, Roger T. Johnson, and Karl A. Smith

5. High School–College Partnerships: Conceptual Models, Programs, and Issues
   Arthur Richard Greenberg

6. Meeting the Mandate: Renewing the College and Departmental Curriculum
   William Toombs and William Tierney

7. Faculty Collaboration: Enhancing the Quality of Scholarship and Teaching
   Ann E. Austin and Roger G. Baldwin

8. Strategies and Consequences: Managing the Costs in Higher Education
   John S. Waggaman

1990 ASHE-ERIC Higher Education Reports

1. The Campus Green: Fund Raising in Higher Education
   Barbara E. Brittingham and Thomas R. Pezzullo

2. The Emeritus Professor: Old Rank - New Meaning
   James E. Mauch, Jack W. Birch, and Jack Matthews

3. "High Risk" Students in Higher Education: Future Trends
   Dionne J. Jones and Betty Collier Watson

4. Budgeting for Higher Education at the State Level: Enigma, Paradox, and Ritual
   Daniel T. Layzell and Jan W. Lyddon

5. Proprietary Schools: Programs, Policies, and Prospects
   John B. Lee and Jamie P. Merisotis

6. College Choice: Understanding Student Enrollment Behavior
   Michael B. Paulsen

7. Pursuing Diversity: Recruiting College Minority Students
   Barbara Astone and Elsa Nuñez-Wormack

8. Social Consciousness and Career Awareness: Emerging Link in Higher Education
   John S. Swift, Jr.

1989 ASHE-ERIC Higher Education Reports

1. Making Sense of Administrative Leadership: The 'L' Word in Higher Education
   Estela M. Bensimon, Anna Neumann, and Robert Birnbaum

2. Affirmative Rhetoric, Negative Action: African-American and Hispanic Faculty at Predominantly White Universities
   Valora Washington and William Harvey

3. Postsecondary Developmental Programs: A Traditional Agenda with New Imperatives
   Louise M. Tomlinson

4. The Old College Try: Balancing Athletics and Academics in Higher Education
   John R. Thelin and Lawrence L. Wiseman

5. The Challenge of Diversity: Involvement or Alienation in the Academy?
   Daryl G. Smith

6. Student Goals for College and Courses: A Missing Link in Assessing and Improving Academic Achievement
   Joan S. Stark, Kathleen M. Shaw, and Malcolm A. Lowther

7. The Student as Commuter: Developing a Comprehensive Institutional Response
   Barbara Jacoby

8. Renewing Civic Capacity: Preparing College Students for Service and Citizenship
   Suzanne W. Morse

1988 ASHE-ERIC Higher Education Reports

1. The Invisible Tapestry: Culture in American Colleges and Universities
   George D. Kuh and Elizabeth J. Whitt

2. Critical Thinking: Theory, Research, Practice, and Possibilities
   Joanne Gainen Kurfiss

3. Developing Academic Programs: The Climate for Innovation
   Daniel T. Seymour

4. Peer Teaching: To Teach is To Learn Twice
   Neal A. Whitman

5. Higher Education and State Governments: Renewed Partnership, Cooperation, or Competition?
   Edward R. Hines

6. Entrepreneurship and Higher Education: Lessons for Colleges, Universities, and Industry
   James S. Fairweather

7. Planning for Microcomputers in Higher Education: Strategies for the Next Generation
   Reynolds Ferrante, John Hayman, Mary Susan Carlson, and Harry Phillips

8. The Challenge for Research in Higher Education: Harmonizing Excellence and Utility
   Alan W. Lindsay and Ruth T. Neumann

1987 ASHE-ERIC Higher Education Reports

1. Incentive Early Retirement Programs for Faculty: Innovative Responses to a Changing Environment
   Jay L. Chronister and Thomas R. Kepple, Jr.

2. Working Effectively with Trustees: Building Cooperative Campus Leadership
   Barbara E. Taylor

3. Formal Recognition of Employer-Sponsored Instruction: Conflict and Collegiality in Postsecondary Education
   Nancy S. Nash and Elizabeth M. Hawthorne

4. Learning Styles: Implications for Improving Educational Practices
   Charles S. Claxton and Patricia H. Murrell

5. Higher Education Leadership: Enhancing Skills through Professional Development Programs
   Sharon A. McDade

6. Higher Education and the Public Trust: Improving Stature in Colleges and Universities
   Richard L. Alfred and Julie Weissman

7. College Student Outcomes Assessment: A Talent Development Perspective
   Maryann Jacobi, Alexander Astin, and Frank Ayala, Jr.

8. Opportunity from Strength: Strategic Planning Clarified with Case Examples
   Robert G. Cope

1986 ASHE-ERIC Higher Education Reports

1. Post-tenure Faculty Evaluation: Threat or Opportunity?
   Christine M. Licata

2. Blue Ribbon Commissions and Higher Education: Changing Academe from the Outside
   Janet R. Johnson and Laurence R. Marcus

3. Responsive Professional Education: Balancing Outcomes and Opportunities
   Joan S. Stark, Malcolm A. Lowther, and Bonnie M.K. Hagerty

4. Increasing Students' Learning: A Faculty Guide to Reducing Stress among Students
   Neal A. Whitman, David C. Spendlove, and Claire H. Clark

5. Student Financial Aid and Women: Equity Dilemma?
   Mary Moran

6. The Master's Degree: Tradition, Diversity, Innovation
   Judith S. Glazer

7. The College, the Constitution, and the Consumer Student: Implications for Policy and Practice
   Robert M. Hendrickson and Annette Gibbs

8. Selecting College and University Personnel: The Quest and the Question
   Richard A. Kaplowitz

1985 ASHE-ERIC Higher Education Reports

1. Flexibility in Academic Staffing: Effective Policies and Practices
   Kenneth P. Mortimer, Marque Bagshaw, and Andrew T. Masland

2. Associations in Action: The Washington, D.C. Higher Education Community
   Harland G. Bloland

3. And on the Seventh Day: Faculty Consulting and Supplemental Income
   Carol M. Boyer and Darrell R. Lewis

4. Faculty Research Performance: Lessons from the Sciences and Social Sciences
   John W. Creswell

5. Academic Program Review: Institutional Approaches, Expectations, and Controversies
   Clifton F. Conrad and Richard F. Wilson

6. Students in Urban Settings: Achieving the Baccalaureate Degree
   Richard C. Richardson, Jr. and Louis W. Bender

7. Serving More Than Students: A Critical Need for College Student Personnel Services
   Peter H. Garland

8. Faculty Participation in Decision Making: Necessity or Luxury?
   Carol E. Floyd

*Out-of-print. Available through EDRS. Call 1-800-443-ERIC.

ORDER FORM 93-4

Quantity   Amount

_____ Please begin my subscription to the 1993 *ASHE-ERIC Higher Education Reports* at $98.00, 32% off the cover price, starting with Report 1, 1993.   _____

_____ Please send a complete set of the 1992 *ASHE-ERIC Higher Education Reports* at $90.00, 33% off the cover price.   _____

_____ Outside the U.S., add $10.00 per series for postage.   _____

Individual reports are avilable at the following prices:

1993, $18.00	1985 to 1987, $10.00
1990 to 1992, $17.00	1983 and 1984, $7.50
1988 and 1989, $15.00	1980 to 1982, $6.50

SHIPPING: **U.S. Orders:** *For subtotal (before discount) of $50.00 or less, add $2.50. For subtotal over $50.00, add 5% of subtotal. Call for rush service options.* **Foreign Orders:** *$2.50 per book.* **U.S. Subscriptions:** *Included in price.* **Foreign Subscriptions:** *Add $10.00.*

PLEASE SEND ME THE FOLLOWING REPORTS:

Quantity	Report No.	Year	Title	Amount

Subtotal: _____
Shipping: _____
Total Due: _____

Please check one of the following:
☐ Check enclosed, payable to GWU–ERIC.
☐ Purchase order attached ($45.00 minimum).
☐ Charge my credit card indicated below:
   ☐ Visa   ☐ MasterCard

Expiration Date _____

Name _____
Title _____
Institution _____
Address _____
City _____ State _____ Zip _____
Phone _____ Fax _____ Telex _____
Signature _____ Date _____

SEND ALL ORDERS TO:
ASHE-ERIC Higher Education Reports
The George Washington University
One Dupont Circle, Suite 630
Washington, DC 20036-1183
Phone: (202) 296-2597

DATE DUE